Goode's World Atlas, © Copyright 1990 by
Rand McNally & Company, R.L. 89-S-200

Enchantment of the World

INDIA

By Sylvia McNair

Consultant for India: P.P. Karan, Ph.D., Professor of Geography, University of Kentucky, Lexington, Kentucky

Consultant for Reading: Robert L. Hillerich, Ph.D., Bowling Green State University, Bowling Green, Ohio

CHILDRENS PRESS ®
CHICAGO

Fresh ingredients for some of the delicious Indian vegetable curries

Library of Congress Cataloging-in-Publication Data

McNair, Sylvia.
  India / by Sylvia McNair.
    p.   cm. — (Enchantment of the world)
  Summary: Discusses the geography, history, people, and
culture of this multi-faceted country.
  ISBN 0-516-02719-0
  1. India—Juvenile literature. [1. India.]
I. Title. II. Series.
DS407.M39 1990
954—dc20   89-25435
                                      CIP
                                       AC

Picture Acknowledgments

The Bettmann Archive: 44 (left), 47 (left), 50, 54 (right), 62 (right); © **BBC Hulton,** 51 (left), 54 (left)
© **Cameramann International Ltd.:** 6 (bottom), 8 (left), 10 (bottom right), 18 (bottom right), 42 (right), 44 (right), 74 (right), 77 (top left, right), 79 (left), 86, 87 (right), 91 (top & bottom left), 93 (top right), 94 (left), 99 (top left), 100 (right), 101 (bottom left), 103 (bottom right), 109 (2 photos), 112 (bottom right), 113 (bottom left)
The Marilyn Gartman Agency: © **Susan Malis,** 87 (left), 93 (bottom right)
© **Virginia Grimes:** 69, 79 (right), 100 (left)
H. Armstrong Roberts: © **Geopress,** 10 (top), 110 (left); © **Koene,** 28 (left), 95 (left), 101 (top); © **Haimer,** 99 (bottom)
Historical Picture Service, Chicago: 38 (left), 61 (left), 62 (left), 68 (bottom), 72 (2 photos); © **Gopal Chitra Kutira,** 65 (left); © **Raj Gopal,** 68 (top)
Journalism Services all rights reserved 1989: © **Steve Vidler,** 5, 27 (left), 33 (left), 45, 93 (top left)
North Wind Picture Archives: 25, 42 (left, center), 51 (right), 52 (2 photos), 55 (2 photos), 58

© **Photri:** 6 (top), 10 (bottom left), 14 (2 photos), 18 (bottom left), 20 (bottom), 22, 28 (right), 30 (right), 31, 33 (right), 46 (right), 74 (left), 80 (bottom), 83, 84 (right), 91 (right), 112 (left), 113 (right), 114 (top), 115 (left, center); © **Les Riess,** 88 (bottom right)
Root Resources: © **Bryon Crader,** 20 (top); © **Jane M. Kriete,** 96 (left), 104 (right); © **Russel A. Kriete,** 96 (right); © **Jane P. Downton,** 101 (right)
Shostal Associates/SuperStock International, Inc.: 16 (2 photos), 30 (left), 46 (left), 77 (bottom left), 82 (left), 89 (bottom), 95 (top right), 99 (top right), 108 (2 photos), 112 (top right), 113 (top left); © **Manley Photo-Tuscon, Ariz,** 13; © **Hubertus Kanus,** 47 (right), 98 (2 photos); © **J. David Day,** 80 (top right)
Tom Stack & Associates: © Steve Elmore, 95 (bottom right), 102 (right); © **Nancy Adams,** 105 (left)
Tony Stone Worldwide-Click/Chicago: © **Hilarie Kavanagh,** Cover, 106 (right), 115 (right); © **David Hanson,** 4; © **Cathlyn Melloan,** 18 (top left), 94 (right); © **Leonard Lee Rue III,** 27 (right); © **Robert Frerck,** 35 (right), 88 (left), 97 (2 photos), 103 (top left & right), 106 (bottom left); © **David Austen,** 80 (top left); © **Trevor Wood,** 102 (left); © **Chris Haigh,** 110 (right); © **David Sutherland,** 114 (bottom)
SuperStock International, Inc.: 8 (right), 18 (top right), 35 (left), 78, 103 (bottom left), 104 (left)
Third Coast Stock Source: © **Scott Housum,** 82 (right), 84 (left)
UPI/Bettmann Newsphotos: 61 (right), 62 (center), 65 (right), 71
Valan: © **K. Ghani,** 17, 88 (top right), 105 (right), 106 (top left); © **B. Templeman,** 38 (right), 40; © **Fred Bruemmer,** 89 (top)
Len W. Meents: Maps on pages 93, 96, 99
Courtesy Flag Research Center, Winchester, Massachusetts 01890: Flag on back cover
Cover: The Taj Mahal

Women from Rajasthan

TABLE OF CONTENTS

The crowded city streets of India are full of interesting sights, sounds, and smells.
Above: The Mahatma Gandhi Road in Calcutta   Below: A bustling market in Hyderabad

Chapter 1

BHARAT MATA,
MOTHER INDIA

India is one of the world's oldest civilizations and one of its youngest independent democracies. The name bring thoughts of strange sights, sounds, and smells. Most of us know so little about her, yet both our past and our future are intertwined.

India seems so complex, so different, so vast. How can an outsider understand a country with more than forty-five hundred years of history and over 800,000,000 people who speak hundreds of different dialects? How can they even understand each other? And what do we in the English-speaking world have in common with them, anyway?

Quite a few things, when you stop to think about it. In the first place, Christopher Columbus would never have come to the Western Hemisphere if he had not been looking for a route to India. Indeed, he thought he had found it, and the natives of the New World have been called Indians ever since as a result of his error.

Trading ships made regular voyages between the American colonies and India for many years before the American

The varied Indian landscape:
Left: The magnificent
Jog Falls in Karnataka
Above: Ladakh, called the
"moonland," an arid area
with unbearable heat
during the day and
extreme cold at night

Revolution. Diplomatic relations were established by President George Washington, who sent an American consul to Calcutta in 1782.

Great Britain, of course, played a long role in the history of India.

Philosophical thought has traveled back and forth between India and English-speaking lands, each influencing the other.

Prominent American and British writers of the nineteenth century were well educated in Indian literature. Ralph Waldo Emerson, Henry David Thoreau, Amos Bronson Alcott, John Greenleaf Whittier, Herman Melville, and Walt Whitman from America and Rudyard Kipling from Britain were fascinated by India and Indian writings. Kipling was born in Bombay and he is well known for his children's classics set in India. Mark Twain wrote, "India is the only foreign land I ever daydream about or deeply long to see again."

India's modern leaders, in turn, were influenced by British and American thought. India's first prime minister, Jawaharlal Nehru, read English and American literature and history widely. So did India's premier poet, Rabindranath Tagore.

Mahatma Gandhi, the Indian hero who deserves most of the credit for leading his country to independence, used nonviolent resistance to tyranny and oppression. His ideas were influenced by both the Hindu religion and the writings of the American essayist Henry David Thoreau.

And in the 1960s, the American Civil Rights Movement derived much of its inspiration from India's experience. The movement's principal leader, the Reverend Martin Luther King, Jr., visited India, met Prime Minister Nehru, and studied Gandhi's methods intensively. Dr. King's birthday is noted each year in India with newspaper editorials that point out what the two countries have learned from one another in their struggles for freedom.

So let us explore this ancient and colorful land together, from its lofty snow-covered Himalayan Mountains to the shores of the Indian Ocean. Let us enjoy her exotic beauty and honor her amazing history.

Above: Quilon is a port on the Indian Ocean and the starting point of a stretch of inland waters. Below: Sand dunes in the Indian desert
Below right: A beach on the Indian Ocean at Trivandrum

Chapter 2

THE LAND AND
THE PEOPLE

India is shaped roughly like a diamond pointing down into ocean waters. The distance from the northern to the southern tip of the diamond is about 2,000 miles (3,219 kilometers). It is almost the same distance across the country from east to west. It is commonly referred to as a subcontinent, because it is so large and because it is separated from the rest of Asia by the highest mountains on earth. Its area of 1,269,219 square miles (3,287,263 square kilometers) makes it the seventh-largest nation in the world. Within its boundaries are rocky plains and vast deserts, jungles and rain forests, coastlines bordered partially by cliffs and partially by sandy beaches, gigantic snow-topped mountains, and huge stretches of fertile farmland.

INDIA'S NEIGHBORS

India's boundaries are extremely irregular, and some of them seem almost always to be a source of dispute with the country's neighbors. Some of those neighbors are kingdoms and some are Socialist republics. On the northwestern border is the Islamic Republic of Pakistan, which was a part of India until 1947. The Democratic Republic of Afghanistan touches a very short strip of India's border at the northern point of the diamond.

The People's Republic of China and the Kingdom of Nepal border on the northeastern face of India's diamond. Toward the east the People's Republic of Bangladesh, a country formed in 1971, has been cut out of the diamond; the land remaining in eastern India is shaped like a hook. The Kingdom of Bhutan, the People's Republic of China, and Burma (renamed the Socialist Republic of Myanma in 1989) lie along this eastern hook.

The southern peninsula is bounded by water — the Bay of Bengal to the east, the Arabian Sea to the west, and the great Indian Ocean to the south. The coastline, including island territories, is 4,252 miles (6,843 kilometers) long. A short 31 miles (50 kilometers) off the southeastern tip of the peninsula is another neighbor, the Democratic Socialist Republic of Sri Lanka, a small island formerly called Ceylon.

Three distinctly different landforms stretch horizontally across India; the Himalaya Mountains in the north; the flat Indo-Gangetic Plain in the central part; and the Deccan, a high plateau that covers most of the southern peninsula.

THE HIMALAYA MOUNTAINS

The Himalaya are the highest and among the oldest mountains in the world, often called the top of the world. Many peaks rise more than 20,000 feet (6,096 meters) toward the sky. India's tallest peak is Nanda Devi, 25,645 feet (7,817 meters) in height, and the tallest mountain, Kanchenjunga, is 28,208 feet (8,598 meters).

Three huge parallel Himalayan ranges form natural walls across 1,500 miles (2,414 kilometers) between the Tibetan region of China and northern India. Many high passes cut through the mountains, studded with glaciers and snow covered for much of

Opposite page: The Himalaya Mountains and Kanchenjunga, seen from Darjeeling

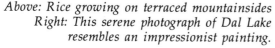

Above: Rice growing on terraced mountainsides
Right: This serene photograph of Dal Lake
resembles an impressionist painting.

the year. Fertile valleys and wide plateaus are hidden among the peaks. Rice paddies color the valley with deep, rich green. Orchards of fruit and nut trees, neat gardens, and cool blue lakes add to the beauty.

Tropical plants grow at the lower elevations of the Himalaya; forests and crops common in temperate climates cover slopes at slightly higher locations.

THE INDO-GANGETIC PLAIN

The vast plains of northern India cover about 300,000 square miles (777,000 square kilometers), and they are home to one of the greatest concentrations of people on earth. Not a single small hill is in sight in this entire region.

Three great rivers, the Indus, the Ganges (or Ganga), and the Brahmaputra, bring fertile soil down from the mountains to enrich the land and supply water for irrigation. Huge seasonal storms, called monsoons, cause the rivers to flood, depositing rich silt on the farmlands. This region is the world's largest alluvial plain, the name given to flat land formed from soil carried by rivers.

Not all of the plains are fertile and pleasant. In the west much of the land in the state of Rajasthan is arid—little more than a desert. Nomadic tribes eke out a living by following their herds of sheep and goats from one watering hole to another.

In the east is the great Ganges River and its tributaries, considered sacred by Hindus. A bath in the holy waters is believed to wash away a person's sins. A devout Hindu tries to make a pilgrimage to sacred places along the Ganges at least once in his or her lifetime.

THE SOUTHERN PENINSULA

The southern peninsula of India is separated from the northern plains by another group of mountains, the 4,000-foot (1,219-meter) Vindhya Range. Two other ranges, rugged but small by comparison with the Himalaya, rise along the coastlines—the Eastern and Western Ghats.

Inside the triangle formed by these mountains is the huge Deccan Plateau. This is a drier region, where successful farming depends upon irrigation. Hot, blistering sun bakes the soil each spring, and strong winds blow the dry earth away. Then the monsoons bring meager precipitation.

There are natural resources in the Deccan, however, rich black soil used for cotton growing and dry forests populated with large animals.

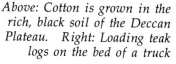

Above: Cotton is grown in the rich, black soil of the Deccan Plateau. Right: Loading teak logs on the bed of a truck

A narrow coastline between the sea and the mountains of the southern peninsula has rich soil and a wet climate that support great stands of sandalwood and teak trees. Elephants roam wild in these forests.

Coastal shipping is well-developed along India's shores. Although there are few good natural harbors, southern India has been a crossroads for traders from many countries for thousands of years.

CLIMATE

There are three seasons in most of India: cold, hot, and rainy. The winter season runs from November to February. Temperatures at that time of year are generally 70 degrees Fahrenheit (21.1 degrees Celsius) and above in the south, in the

Elephants roam the forests of the southern peninsula

60s (15.5 to 21 degrees Celsius) in the plains, and 40s and below (4.4 degrees Celsius and below) in the highlands.

The hot season, March to May, is generally dry, windy, and dusty, with temperatures rising to above 100 degrees Fahrenheit (37.7 degrees Celsius) in the plains. Higher elevations in southern India are a little cooler, but humid. Hill stations in the Himalaya also are cool and pleasant.

The monsoon season starts in June and continues through September. It brings cooler temperatures and badly needed water, but devastating floods in the Ganges valley often cause much destruction and loss of life during this time of year. After the monsoons pass, cool weather begins in October.

THE INDIAN PEOPLE

Who are the Indian people? They represent centuries of immigration into the subcontinent from many other lands. Some

The many shades of color of the Indian people reflect centuries of immigration to the subcontinent.

are light skinned while others are dark. They are short and tall, thin and stocky. Most people in northern India have descended from pale-skinned people from Europe and the Middle East who came into India through passes in the western mountains. In southern India the people have darker pigmentation. They are called Dravidians—descendants of people who were settled in the Indus valley and were pushed south by the Indo-European people.

There are two things the great majority of Indians have in common: 83 percent of them are Hindus, and about 80 percent of them either live in, or have roots in, small villages. Beyond that, the diversity is almost unimaginable.

India's first prime minister, Jawaharlal Nehru, said, "There is no such thing as an Indian. One is either a Punjabi, a Gujarati, a Tamil, or a Kashmiri, and then an Indian." In other words, most of the country's residents identify themselves first with their region or state, such as Punjab or Kashmir. Their identity as Indians is secondary. This is especially obvious in language.

At least 225 separate regional dialects are spoken in India, representing 16 major languages. Hindi is the official language; English is called the associate official language. Explorers, nomads, and settlers who came into India from far-off lands brought their native languages with them. Experts in the development of languages sort India's bewildering mixture of tongues into four major groups: Indo-European, Dravidian, Austro-Asiatic, and Tibeto-Burman.

Hindi is spoken by about 40 percent of the Indian people. It is derived from Sanskrit, an ancient language that originated in India. Many European languages—Greek, Latin, English, German, and others—have words with Sanskrit roots. Literature written in Sanskrit dates back to about 1000 B.C. Hindi literature began to develop in the thirteenth century A.D.

Tamil and three other languages of the Dravidian family are spoken by the people of southern India. A body of literature written in these languages has existed for more than two thousand years. Tamil is probably one of the oldest languages in the world.

A few isolated tribal groups who live in eastern and central India speak dialects that belong to the Austro-Asiatic language family, and a few other tribes living near the borders of Tibet and Burma speak dialects derived from the languages of those countries, the Tibeto-Burman group.

India's diversities make it an especially fascinating country to study, and an impossible one to understand completely. But as the world's largest democracy and one of the world's oldest civilizations, it is certainly of great importance to all of us.

Chapter 3

ANCIENT INDIA

In one sense, India is one of the youngest nations in the world. Only in the twentieth century, in 1947, independence from Great Britain was achieved and India became a member of the British Commonwealth. But the Indian civilization is one of the oldest on earth. Its roots can be traced back for more than forty-five hundred years. Before then, our knowledge of history disappears into the mysteries of a forgotten past.

India, historically, included the territories now known as Pakistan and Bangladesh. Its name comes from the life-giving Indus River, the source of water for one of the largest irrigation systems in the world. The Indus originates in Tibet, flows across northern India into Pakistan, and empties into the Arabian Sea.

PRE-ARYAN CULTURES

We know about two very early groups of people who lived in India. They are known as pre-Aryan cultures. The northern group is called the Indus valley culture or the Harappan culture. Those who lived in the central and southern sections of the Indian peninsula are called the Dravidians.

Opposite page, top: The oldest shrine in India was built in the third century before the Christian era at Kanchipuram. Bottom: Ruins of the Indus valley civilization

The ancient city of Mohenjodaro was built along the Indus River in present-day Pakistan.

Very little is known about the Dravidians, but scholars have discovered quite a lot about the people of the Indus valley. The remains of two ancient cities were uncovered by archaeologists in the 1920s. Harappa and Mohenjodaro were built along the Indus River, within the boundaries of present-day Pakistan. The Indus valley civilization that centered on these cities was thriving from about 2500 to 1600 B.C.

Harappa was a great city, encircled by thick brick walls, 3.5 miles (5.6 kilometers) in circumference. It was the capital of a very large territory, a triangle about 1,000 miles (1,609 kilometers) long on each side. More than five hundred other villages, cities, and seaports were within the triangle. There were farming communities, trading centers, and ports with well-equipped shipping facilities. A lively trade was carried on with cities of the Middle East. The Harappan merchants exported copper, gold, ivory, cotton, timber, and precious stones.

Both of these capital cities were laid out in a neat geometric pattern. Avenues and streets were lined with brick houses, shops, and restaurants. Homes were arranged around courtyards. Indoor baths and toilets were connected to a sanitary sewage system.

The arts were well developed, too. Glazed pottery of the period was elaborately decorated and well designed. It is evident that Harappa had a strong, prosperous middle class.

Archaeologists have found, among other objects, more than a thousand small seals—soapstone pieces only about the size of a postage stamp, elaborately carved with figures of animals and symbols. They may have been used to mark goods for shipment, designating the contents of bags or possibly identifying the exporter. In any case, they represent an unsolved riddle. No one has yet been able to decode the symbols.

Another riddle, even more baffling, is why this highly developed civilization simply disappeared after about a thousand years of achievement and prosperity. Mohenjodaro appears to have declined slowly. All of its artworks and even its buildings began to be of a much lower quality than they had been formerly. The Harappan culture, however, evidently ended quite abruptly.

It may have been physical forces that brought them down, such as floods, droughts, or land shifts. Or perhaps, as some historians believe, the old culture was wiped out by an invasion of light-skinned nomads from Central Asia.

THE ARYAN PERIOD, OR VEDIC AGE

The word "Aryan" has been misused, especially by Adolf Hitler, who tried to claim that there is a pure Aryan race. At one time in the far-distant past, there were people who could be called Aryans, but today the word is used correctly only to identify a large family of languages. Included in that group are languages spoken by a great many of the world's people today: Italian, Greek, German, English, Celtic, Iranian, and Hindi.

The ancient Aryans were wandering herders. They left very little behind them to give us any clue as to their history—no cities, sculpture, pottery, or even burial grounds. The only concrete evidence of the long period of their domination in India, which started about 1500 B.C. and continued for more than five hundred years, is a body of sacred literature, the *Vedas*. These are the world's oldest religious writings, and they explain in detail the foundations of Hinduism.

Other great scriptural literature, such as the Bible, are of enormous value to students of history. They contain accounts of historical events, kings and kingdoms, military campaigns, and even detailed genealogical charts of important leaders. The Vedas, in contrast, tell us about the ways of life of the Indians and how the universe originated. Sun worship is important in the Veda. As the discovery of fire was a very significant step in human history, one of the four Vedas considers fire to be a god.

They tell us about sacrifices to the gods and the religious rituals. They tell us that Vedic Aryan society consisted of three functionally based classes of people: nobles, priests, and ordinary people. These classes were not rigidly segregated; they could eat together, marry outside the hereditary class, and change occupations. In later writings a fourth class is mentioned, the warriors.

Over the centuries the wandering tribes constantly fought one another. Separate kingdoms evolved, and each king recruited a

Alexander the Great overthrew Darius III and opened up land and sea routes between Europe and the subcontinent.

standing army. Priests gradually developed more elaborate religious rituals, and at the same time they increased their power over society until they held the highest rank of all.

MORE INVASIONS

Indian history becomes a little clearer along the sixth and fifth centuries B.C., because certain important events were recorded in the writings of various people.

King Darius I of Persia invaded northwest India in 518 B.C. and made the Indus valley and west Punjab part of his vast empire. He took great amounts of wealth from the territory, in the form of tribute, or taxes. Stories of India's riches soon reached Europe.

In 327 B.C., Alexander the Great of Macedonia overthrew Darius III and took his armies across the Indus River. He was met with strong resistance, however, and was forced to retreat. As a result of Alexander's Indian campaign, both land and sea routes were opened up between Europe and the subcontinent.

Chapter 4

INDIA'S RELIGIONS

Why has Indian civilization survived intact for nearly five thousand years in spite of invasion after invasion by many different kinds of people from many different lands, many of them hostile and warlike? Scholars use the word *syncretism* to explain it. It means, simply, the combination of different beliefs and practices. The people of India have had an unusual ability to absorb different ideas and customs, to syncretize them into their own way of life. This is especially true when it comes to religion.

In order to understand India's history, it is necessary to examine the religions of this great land. Two of the world's foremost religions, Hinduism and Buddhism, were born in India, as were the two uniquely Indian religions of Jainism and Sikhism. Islam and Christianity were brought into the country by foreigners; they are important minority religions. A few Indians, called Parsis, follow an ancient Persian religion founded by Zoroaster in the sixth century B.C. There also are two ancient Jewish communities more than a thousand years old.

HINDUISM

Hinduism is the most important religion in India. By the end of the Vedic Age, Hinduism had become the basic element in Indian society. Westerners find it hard to understand Hinduism. It is a

Left: Hindu temples are ornate and very colorful.   Right: A Hindu holy man

complex social system and a body of ideas and has been the foundation of Indian culture for four thousand years. For the most orthodox Hindus, there are rules determining nearly every aspect of daily life.

Hinduism is not a church in the sense that Westerners understand the word. There is no formal structure or group of leaders to run an organization. There is not even an established set of beliefs or creeds.

But there is religion within Hinduism, more than one religion, in fact. A Hindu can hold any of various beliefs; he or she can even be an atheist or agnostic and still be accepted as a Hindu.

A most basic part of Hindu tradition is the caste system, and even that is constantly changing and, in some parts of the country, becoming less important. Vedic writings name four functionally based classes, or castes, of people: *brahmans* (priests and scholars),

Above: In the Brahman section of Jodhpur, the buildings are painted blue. Left: A Hindu temple in Varanasi covered with intricate carving

kshatriyas (warriors and rulers), *vaisyas* (tradespeople and farmers), and *sudras* (servants and ordinary workers). Over the centuries these four simple classes have become split into several thousand castes. Each caste is expected to observe its own traditional *dharma*, or moral duty. In some cases it is a specific occupation that defines a caste. In other cases a group of people who adapt new or different religious ideas may become a separate caste. Certain rules governing intermarriage, diet, and ceremonial observations keep the castes separated from one another.

The Vedas mention only the four major castes, but at some point during the Aryan Period, a fifth group, a sort of "non-caste," emerged. These were people who performed tasks too lowly even for the sudras. They tanned animal hides, swept up the grounds where dead persons had been cremated, and did other jobs considered unclean. They were called "untouchables." They were not allowed to have any contact with the rest of Hindu society. They could not drink from the same wells, live in the same neighborhoods, or even enter the temples. Some people felt they were contaminated even by the shadow of an untouchable.

Mahatma Gandhi, the great popular leader who had so much influence over twentieth-century India, insisted that untouchability was wrong and should be wiped out. It has been abolished by the national constitution and its practice in any form is forbidden. Untouchability still exists in India, especially in some remote rural areas, but attitudes are changing.

In large cities, where middle-class Indians are exposed to Western ideas and customs, some of the caste rules appear to be lessening. Modern industry requires many people to go into occupations that were unknown to former generations. Thus workers do, in effect, move outside their hereditary caste. But in rural areas the old ways are still strong.

Three interlocking elements are basic to Hinduism: dharma, *karma*, and *reincarnation*. First, one should live according to his or her own dharma, the moral duties appropriate to one's station in life. Secondly, Hindus believe that everything a person does has a consequence, that eventually good deeds will be rewarded and sins will be punished. This is karma, and it is regarded as a natural law. An equally important belief is reincarnation, or rebirth. Each person is believed to live several lives before achieving a final supreme goal, when all evils and all earthly desires have been overcome. Both good and bad deeds have an effect on a person's happiness or misery in future lives as well as in the present one.

Hinduism is *polytheistic*; that is, it recognizes many gods and

*The Nandi Bull (above) and the Goddess of War (right)
represent two of the many Hindu gods and goddesses.*

goddesses. The three most important are: Brahma, the creator;
Vishnu, the preserver; and Shiva, the destroyer. Each of these has
a consort (spouse), and Vishnu had a variety of previous
incarnations. Thousands of legends have developed about the
gods. Many Hindus believe that all the traditional gods and
goddesses are really different forms of one supreme being.

JAINISM

In the sixth century B.C. a young Hindu named Vardhamana
was born, the son of a wealthy and powerful chief who lived in
northern India. He had a questioning nature, and when he was
thirty years old and his parents had died, he decided to leave his
life of ease and become an ascetic—a person who practices self-
denial as a means of discipline and purification of the spirit. For
twelve years Vardhamana wandered about the country meditating
and debating the meaning of life and death with other ascetics.

As he gained confidence in the ideas that had come to him, he

Although the followers of Jainism are small in number, their temples are elaborate, such as this one in Calcutta.

became a persuasive preacher. His disciples called him *Mahavira*, the Great Hero, or *Jina*, the Conqueror. From Jina came the name of a new religion, Jainism, the religion of the conquerors.

Mahavira accepted the fundamentals of Hinduism, such as the concepts of karma and reincarnation, but he reinterpreted them. He taught that the purpose of life is to cleanse the soul by getting rid of earthly desires and abstaining from all evil behavior. He believed that every living thing has a soul, and that killing any living thing is the greatest evil of all.

Jainism does not believe in a personal God. It believes that perfect wisdom can be attained through right faith, right knowledge, and right conduct. Right conduct means, above all, nonviolence. Jains carry nonviolence to such an extreme that they avoid killing anything at all. They cannot be farmers, since cultivating the soil will kill creatures living in the earth. They carry small brooms with them to sweep away any tiny insects they might step on and wear cloth face masks to avoid killing any germs through breathing. "Nonviolence is the supreme religion," is a Jain motto adopted by Mahatma Gandhi.

Less than half of one percent are followers of the Jain religion.

31

BUDDHISM

Buddhism is the fourth-largest religion in the world and the largest in several Asian countries. While it is practiced by only a handful of people in India today, its roots are purely Indian. Through Buddhism, many Indian ideas and practices have spread throughout such countries as Burma, Thailand, Cambodia, Sri Lanka, Nepal, China, Mongolia, Korea, and Japan.

Siddhartha Gautama, who came to be known as the Buddha, lived at about the same time as Mahavira. He, too, was born in the foothills of the Himalaya. He, too, was the son of a wealthy tribal lord. He was a gifted scholar and athlete, and his family's life-style was comfortable, even extravagant.

Like Mahavira, Gautama became dissatisfied with his easy life and at the age of twenty-nine he, too, became an ascetic. After several years of self-denial, study, and meditation, he came to a new understanding of life, which he called Enlightenment. For forty years he traveled from village to village, preaching a message of love, compassion, tolerance, and self-restraint. As he died, he gave a final message:

> A Buddha can only point the way. Become a
> lamp unto yourself. Work out your own
> salvation diligently.

Buddha considered himself a teacher, but after his death some of his followers began to deify him, to call him a savior.

Buddhist philosophy, art, and poetry became widespread in India. Masterpieces of architecture, sculpture, and painting still exist, illustrating India's Buddhist heritage.

The Jami Masjid Mosque in Delhi (left) and the richly decorated interior of the Sakyamuni Lotsawa Buddhist Temple (right)

As a religion, Buddhism never attracted a large proportion of the Indian population, but its teachings of compassion and nonviolence became an integral part of Indian thought and character. In a sense Hinduism took over Buddhism in India and absorbed it: the brahmans eventually declared that Buddha was the ninth incarnation of Vishnu, the Hindu Preserver god. The process of syncretism was at work again.

Buddhism was thoroughly Indian in its conception, and India is still strongly influenced by the teachings of the Buddha.

ISLAM

Islam (submission to God) was founded by an Arab named Muhammad, who was born in A.D. 570. Followers of this religion are called Muslims (those who have submitted to God). It is the second-largest religious group in modern India; about 11 percent of the country's population are Muslims.

In Muhammad's Arabia, people worshiped many gods and idols. He taught the revolutionary idea that there is only one God, whom he called Allah. He had a vision in which the angel Gabriel came to him and told him to preach a new religion to others in his country. He taught equality, brotherhood, compassion, and mercy. Before he died, Muhammad became a political and military leader as well as a religious one.

After his death in A.D. 632, Muhammad's followers set out to carry the message of Islam by force to neighboring lands. By 670, they had conquered Iraq, Iran, Turkey, and all of northern Africa.

Muslims made raids into India from time to time over the next few centuries. Arabian Muslims came in the eighth century, Turkish in the twelfth. In 1206 Delhi was occupied by Muslim sultans (kings), and from there they worked their way east and south. They converted low-caste Hindus to Islam.

Mughal is the Indian word for Mongol, a person from the north Asian country of Mongolia. The meaning changed over the years, and today it refers to Islamic Mughals who ruled India from 1526 to 1707. The English version of the word, *mogul*, means a very important person, a magnate, or an autocrat.

The Mughals displaced the weak sultans in 1526. The greatest of the Mughal rulers was Akbar, who attempted to reconcile differences between the Hindus and the Muslims. During this period Hindu and Muslim traditions interacted and together made important achievements in poetry, music, and architecture. The Muslim rule collapsed after over 550 years and was replaced by the British.

But in the twentieth century, tensions between Muslims and Hindus led to the division of India into two countries. Pakistan is now an Islamic state, while India is a secular state where Hindus are in the majority but followers of Islam practice their religion freely.

Left: The Golden Temple, the center of Sikh worship, is made with bronze plates that are covered with pure gold leaf. Right: A Sikh guard at the Golden Temple

SIKHISM

A man named Nanak lived in the Punjab region of northwestern India at the end of the fifteenth century and beginning of the sixteenth century. This was a region where Muslims and Hindus came into close contact, and Nanak was interested in the similarities in the two religions. He was a Hindu himself, but he had close Muslim friends and knew quite a bit about their beliefs. He visited Hindu holy places and made a pilgrimage to Mecca as well.

Nanak began to question traditional Eastern religions at the same time in history that Martin Luther, in Europe, was questioning the practices of medieval Christianity. Nanak began to preach a new message of one universal god and a brotherhood that would unite Muslims and all castes of Hindus. His followers called themselves *Sikhs*, from a Sanskrit word meaning disciple.

Later Sikhs were persecuted by Muslims, and in self-defense they established a political state and took part in military skirmishes.

Today about 2.5 percent of India's population are Sikhs. Most of them live in Punjab and are farmers and herders. Their principal shrine, the Golden Temple, is at Amritsar. The holy scripture is called *Granth Sahib*, the *Book of the Lord*.

Sikhs believe strongly in one god and are opposed to the caste system. They also accept the Hindu ideas of karma and rebirth, and everyday rituals and practices are much like those of the Hindus. Intermarriage between the two groups is common.

At the same time, Sikhs have their own identity. All Sikh men use the last name Singh. They wear a steel bangle on the right wrist as a religious symbol. They are generally tall in stature; they wear tightly braided beards and cover their long hair with turbans.

CHRISTIANITY

About 3 percent of India's people are Christian, most of them living in the south. Many people in that part of the country believe that Saint Thomas, one of Christ's apostles, spent some time in India and died here. Other traditions tell of early Christian settlements.

Saint Francis Xavier was the first Christian missionary to India. He came in 1542. Ten years later he died and was buried here. Missionaries from Portugal and other Catholic countries followed him. Protestants arrived in the eighteenth century.

Christian efforts have influenced education, medicine, and social reform in India. Christian ideas, too, have had an effect on the thinking of such prominent Indians as Mahatma Gandhi and the modern poet Rabindranath Tagore.

Chapter 5

INDIAN AND
MUGHAL EMPIRES

Shortly after the defeat of Alexander the Great and his Greek and Macedonian forces, in about 322 B.C., the first great Indian empire, the Maurya Dynasty, was founded. Chandragupta, the first emperor, conquered and ruled over large areas. His son Bindusara and his grandson Asoka enlarged the empire until it covered nearly all of the subcontinent. The Maurya Dynasty ruled for about 135 years.

During this period the government was well organized and efficiently administered. There was a large army and a secret police. Punishment for crimes was severe. All land was owned by the government; peasants who farmed the land had to pay huge taxes.

The Mauryan period was one of great splendor at court. The rulers and nobles lived surrounded by luxury. They dressed in great finery and wore elaborate golden jewelry encrusted with diamonds, pearls, rubies, and sapphires. Their palaces were equally extravagant, decorated with elaborate carvings and inlaid with gems. Murals that have survived to modern times illustrate these elegant details.

A section of Asoka's edicts (right) and a shrine to Buddha (far right) built by Asoka

EMPEROR ASOKA

Asoka, the last Mauryan emperor, was a most unusual man. After he had led a successful military conquest, he suddenly became aware of the suffering the fighting had caused and was filled with remorse. From then on he ruled with gentleness and compassion.

Asoka was impressed with the teachings of Buddha, who had died some two hundred years earlier. He proclaimed a number of edicts that were more like sermons than laws. His edicts were carved on stone pillars and on the walls of rocks and caves. They stressed simplicity and kindness to all living images. He believed in *ahimsa* (nonviolence). Asoka himself gave up hunting, which had been a traditional sport of kings. He urged his people to eat a vegetarian diet, in order to avoid the killing of animals.

Apparently Asoka never formally declared himself a Buddhist or promoted that religion openly. If he had, the Hindu brahmans would have reacted strongly. However, he sent Buddhist missionaries to Ceylon (present-day Sri Lanka), Egypt, and other locations.

Asoka said this about religion:

> All sects deserve reverence for one reason or another. By thus acting a man exalts his own sect and at the same time does service to the sects of other people.

INTERNATIONAL TRADE

Asoka lived during the third century B.C. Very little is known about important historic events in India for the next five hundred years after Asoka's death. We do know, however, that Greeks and other invaders made several incursions into northern India. We also know that India became one of the most important trading spots on earth. Cargo-laden ships sailed regularly between southern India and ports in Egypt and Europe.

India had a great many items to sell that were in great demand in Europe. Among them were spices, drugs, sandalwood, cotton, silk, and precious stones. In return for these items, Indian princes were able to acquire gold, wines, arms, fine glass, and porcelain.

THE GUPTA EMPIRE

During the fourth century A.D., India came into another age of greatness. The period from about 320 to 750 is known as the Gupta Age.

The founder of the Gupta Dynasty, Chandragupta I, gained

Ruins of the University of Nalanda, which was a noted university from the fourth to the twelfth centuries

control over much of northern India. His son Samudragupta and his grandson Chandragupta II extended the empire completely across the northern part of India. Like Asoka before him, Chandragupta II was a peaceful and benevolent ruler. He encouraged development of the arts and sciences. The times were prosperous, and during this reign India's achievements in sculpture, painting, literature, and technology made it the most highly civilized country of the time. Masterpieces of poetry and drama were written that have survived.

Several fine universities in northern India attracted students from all over Asia. Indian scientists knew that the earth is round and rotates on its axis—a concept that was still being argued by European scholars nearly a thousand years later.

Indian mathematicians used algebra. They also developed the idea of zero and invented the system of numbers mistakenly called Arabic numerals. In these studies, too, India was centuries ahead of most of the world.

Manufacturing was quite advanced. Smelting processes produced iron of the highest quality.

The Gupta rulers were Hindu, but Hindus and Buddhists were living together peaceably. Many Buddhist temples and shrines were built and they, too, were elaborately and luxuriously decorated.

Indian cultural influence began to spread eastward, into Burma and other lands of southeast Asia. Both trade goods and religion—Hinduism and Buddhism—were exported. To this day, even though Buddhism is the major religion of Thailand, Cambodia, and Laos, and Islam predominates in Malaysia and the Indonesian islands, a layer of Hinduism can still be sensed underneath the surface.

The Gupta Dynasty was eventually overthrown by outside invaders. From the sixth century through the thirteenth century, a succession of invasions and migrations from outside lands rolled over northern India, resulting in political fragmentation. The country was divided into a number of principalities and small states. By the year A.D. 1200, a network of Hindu kingdoms covered the subcontinent.

ISLAM COMES TO THE SUBCONTINENT

Meanwhile, followers of the prophet Muhammad were at work spreading their faith far and wide. They believed fervently in one God and that they should wage "holy war" against infidels (nonbelievers). The first Muslims reached Sind (a province in present-day southern Pakistan) in the year 644, and conquered Sind in 711.

Later on, sultans conducted raids into India from Afghanistan.

*Both Marco Polo (left) and Vasco da Gama (center)
sailed to India to find exotic spices (right).*

The invaders marched through the Khyber Pass in the tenth and
eleventh centuries, looting the wealth of Indian cities and
kidnapping women. Because the Muslim religion forbids the
worship of idols, the warriors smashed or mutilated thousands of
Hindu temple sculptures. Wherever Muslim warriors went, in all
the countries of the Middle East and Far East, they broke noses,
fingers, and toes off ancient statues as a religious protest against
idolatry.

The first Islamic dynasty in South Asia was established in Delhi
in 1206 and lasted for more than three hundred years.

During the same period, three traders from Italy passed through
India on their way to China. The youngest, Marco Polo, wrote
about his travels in the Orient, and his writings were the first
about India to reach Europe. He called the land, "the noblest and
richest country in the world."

Europeans were enthusiastic customers for Indian goods,
especially spices. But travel between Europe and India was
difficult and hazardous, and European merchants had to rely on
Arabian middlemen to transport the valuable cargo across the
mountains and seas. In the late fifteenth century, navigators and
explorers from Europe were looking for new ways to reach "the

Indies.'' Christopher Columbus, backed by Spain, sailed west in 1492, but succeeded in discovering the New World instead of the Orient. Vasco da Gama, a Portuguese sailor, found a route to India by sailing around the southern tip of Africa, then north along Africa's east coast and east across the Indian Ocean.

THE MUGHAL PERIOD

The founder of the Mughal Empire was a Muslim king named Babar who invaded India in 1526. He was part Mongol and came from Afghanistan. Following Babar seven generations of Mughal emperors extended their territories until they included all of northern India, Afghanistan, present-day Pakistan and Bangladesh, and much of southern India.

The collection of small kingdoms that made up India was not yet a nation in modern terms. Their only unifying force was Hinduism. The Mughals did not destroy the kingdoms; they simply established an umbrella government on top of them. Local government and law enforcement were left in local hands. The Mughal emperors demanded only military support and the payment of tribute (money given in return for protection).

The greatest Mughal ruler was Akbar, Babar's grandson, who reigned for forty-nine years. He was a superb administrator who surrounded himself with brilliant advisers.

Akbar knew that he could not control a number of the Hindu holdings unless he brought the smaller Hindu kings over to his side. He managed to do this by permitting them to continue to practice the Hindu religion, to marry Hindu princesses, and by bringing Hindu generals into his court and armies. He recognized the great diversity among the Indian people, and he made reforms

Akbar receiving a foreign visitor (left); the Red Fort in New Delhi, a symbol of Moghul power (right)

in taxes and land use in order to be fair to the different groups.

He stopped the destruction of Hindu temples and artworks and encouraged both Hindu and Muslim artists in their work. Akbar was a patron of poets and encouraged religious scholars to meet together in discussion groups.

Akbar's policies were so wise and successful that the Mughal Empire was able to hold onto its power for one hundred years after his death, even though his successors were not nearly as gifted in administration.

Jahangir, Akbar's son, married a member of the Persian nobility who had great influence over him. Persian became the accepted language at court and among the upper classes. Persian clothing was the fashion; nobles took on Persian names.

Much of this Persian influence can be seen in modern India. Urdu, the popular language today in the Punjab and other parts of northern India, is a mixture of Persian and certain Indian dialects. Jawaharlal Nehru spoke Urdu at home, his first name was Persian, and his clothing—tight trousers and the so-called Nehru jacket—were Muslim styles.

In the arts a style called Indo-Islamic developed, a combination of Persian-Muslim and Hindu. Architecture, painting, and even music became distinctively Mughal.

The Taj Mahal

The greatest example of Mughal art is to be seen in a glorious shrine, the Taj Mahal. This lovely building of gleaming white marble, inlaid with precious stones, was built by Shah Jahan, Jahangir's successor. He built the Taj as a monument and tomb for his beloved wife. Even today, more than three hundred years after it was built, it is considered by many to be the most beautifully designed and decorated structure in the world.

In spite of the glories of the Mughal period and the surface calm between the Muslim and Hindu religions, the two groups remained separate and apart, forever divided by deep, irreconcilable differences in belief. The Muslims held the political power, but India continued to be overwhelmingly Hindu, and life in the villages went on with little change.

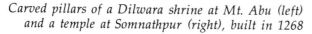

*Carved pillars of a Dilwara shrine at Mt. Abu (left)
and a temple at Somnathpur (right), built in 1268*

INDIA IN THE 1600s

Akbar's successors continued to wage conquests over territories until they controlled nearly all of the Indian subcontinent. These were prosperous times. During the seventeenth century the population of India grew from about 100 million to 150 million; it was probably greater than all of Europe.

Many Europeans visited India during this period, and they discovered that it was one of the most highly developed and civilized countries in the known world. Its buildings were magnificent, and artists and craftspeople were creating works of great elegance.

Trade between India and foreign powers was brisk. Products for export—spices, indigo, sugar, rice, pearls, diamonds, cotton, and silk cloth—were much in demand in Europe. And the balance of trade was in India's favor. Gold and silver bullion came into the country in great quantities, and this flow continued until well into the twentieth century.

Most of India's people still lived in poverty. India was a land

In the seventeenth century rajahs, such as the one in the lithograph (left), lived in great luxury. Temples dominated nearly every village (right).

consisting of a few great cities, with vast rural stretches in between. The villagers knew little or nothing of life as the wealthy lived it or of interaction with foreigners. Each village raised its own food, wheat in the north and west and rice in the east and the south, and was more or less self-sufficient, with its own priest, artisans, shops, and law enforcement.

Magnificent mosques in the big cities were evidence of the Muslim presence, but a Hindu temple dominated nearly every village.

Where did all the precious metals received in trade go? Much was used in the making of intricate jewelry and ornaments; the rest disappeared into the treasuries of the Mughal rulers and the pockets of the merchants.

Sultans and *rajahs* (princes or chiefs) lived extravagantly, surrounded by luxury and showy pomp and ceremony. In contrast, the merchants tried to keep their wealth from public view. The front walls of their homes were drab and ordinary, giving no hint of the beautiful gardens, courtyards, and living quarters hidden behind them.

Chapter 6

THE EAST INDIA COMPANY AND THE BRITISH EMPIRE

When the Portuguese explorer Vasco da Gama arrived in India in 1498, he found lively seaports filled with traders from several Arab lands and Africa, as well as from China and all other parts of Asia. Within two years, six more Portuguese ships arrived.

These first European merchants in India quickly recognized the rich stores of trade goods available in this new marketplace. They bought a warehouse and left more than fifty Portuguese businessmen there to buy and store goods for later shipment to Europe.

Spices were particularly valuable. Pepper, cloves, ginger, and others were in demand for use in preserving food in those days, since refrigeration methods had not yet been developed. Other Indian products included silk and cotton fabrics, indigo, grains, and drugs.

The Portuguese developed friendly trade relations with the Hindu kingdom of southern India. For a time they dominated trade in the Indian Ocean, and the king of Portugal became the richest ruler in Europe.

Other European nations were interested in cashing in on the riches of "the Indies," as all the lands east of Africa came to be called. Spain seized the Portuguese holdings in 1580, but lost them to England a few years later.

THE BRITISH ENTER THE SCENE

In 1600 Queen Elizabeth I of England chartered the East India Company. This act was the beginning of a new era. From that moment on, English thoughts and deeds would influence the course of India's history.

The first ships of the East India Company arrived in India in 1608. Traders were called "factors" in English, and warehouses where trade goods were stored were known as "factories." The English factors found great quantities of treasure available for purchase, but the Indians had little interest in anything from Europe except gold and silver.

The East India Company quickly established trading stations in Indian ports. Soon the English had control over trade in the Arabian Sea and the Persian Gulf, and before long they expanded to India's east coast.

The Indians found one important difference between the English on the one hand and the Spanish and Portuguese on the other. Jesuit priests had accompanied the Spanish and Portuguese traders, with the purpose of converting Hindus to Christianity. The English, however, were content to ignore religious matters in dealing with the Indians.

All through the 1600s the Mughals still held political control over much of the subcontinent, but their governments were getting weaker. Incompetent leadership, parochial policies, and

The English fort of Bombay

high taxation imposed on Hindus were the main causes of the decline of the great Mughal period.

At the same time, English businessmen were quietly gaining strongholds on both coasts. They leased land at strategic places near ports and established fortifications to protect the company's property. Indian traders settled nearby, where they could trade with and be protected by the company. Good-sized Indian cities grew up around the English forts, such as Calcutta, Madras, and Bombay.

Bombay Island was owned by Portugal, and when Charles II of England married a Portuguese princess he acquired the island as a part of her dowry. The company leased it from the king in 1668, and it was the only land in India actually owned by the British crown for the next two centuries.

A provincial governor during the Mughal period was called a *nawab*, a word derived from both Hindi and Urdu. The word has come into the English language as "nabob," meaning a person of great wealth and prominence.

*Above: East India Company troops marched in review
before an Indian prince.
Right: The facade of the old East India House*

THE RISE OF THE EAST INDIA COMPANY

During the eighteenth century the small, weak Indian
principalities were constantly quarreling with one another. The
East India Company took advantage of the situation and
encouraged the tribal warfare. By the 1750s the company had
become the most important power in the land. Before long it was
acting as the government of the huge subcontinent of India. It
collected taxes, recruited armies, and waged war against the
neighboring lands of Afghanistan, Burma, and Nepal.

How did the company take over an entire country? Several
actions contributed to its success.

The English agents seized every opportunity to negotiate
diplomatic alliances with weak Mughal leaders and local princes,
promising to give them protection from internal and external
enemies. In return, company agents were granted the right to
collect taxes in order to pay the soldiers and policemen.

Lord Charles Cornwallis (above) and soldiers who were in the service of the East India Company (right)

Native Indians were recruited to serve as mercenary soldiers to guard company fortifications and to help company allies stay in power. These soldiers, called *sepoys* in Hindi, were trained well, paid regularly, and given uniforms to wear. All this gave the soldiers a sense of importance and assured loyalty to their employers.

Between 1757 and 1759 the East India Company acquired territories around Calcutta by defeating one of the local rulers in Bengal. The British took advantage of the internal divisions and subdued most of the local rulers by playing one against the other in a policy of "divide and rule." Within twenty years all of the Ganges valley was under company rule. By 1849 Sikhs were subjugated in the Punjab.

One of the early governor-generals of the East India Company was Lord Charles Cornwallis, the commanding officer whose surrender to American forces at Yorktown, Virginia, in 1781, ended the American revolutionary war. He was sent to India in 1786, where he served for seven years.

Cornwallis brought about two reforms that had far-reaching effects in India. He laid the foundation for the Indian Civil Service by paying employees of the company properly and supervising them well. Then he turned land over to large farmers, permitting them to become landlords. These farmers became India's first real middle class. Their sons and grandsons were able to get a good Western education, and eventually they became leaders of modern India.

British opinions on how best to manage Indian affairs differed greatly, both among the Englishmen employed there by the company and among the politicians at home. Some felt that the Indians should be left alone as much as possible as long as British business interests were protected. Some believed that the only answer to the many problems would be for England to control India completely. Some company agents were opportunists, interested above all in gaining wealth and power for themselves. Some genuinely loved the Indian people; others were outspoken bigots.

By 1818, after years of skirmishes and battles in many different parts of the country, the British had established control over most of the subcontinent. About half the land was directly governed by the British governor-general; the rest continued to be ruled by Indian princes who acknowledged their dependence on Britain as a superior power.

In the two hundred years since the East India Company was founded, England had made great progress toward becoming a world power. Her economy was expanding as a result of the start of the Industrial Revolution. India, on the other hand, had lost ground from the height of its development in the 1600s. Constant warfare, incompetent leadership, and theft of its wealth by greedy and extravagant princes and overlords had turned it into a weak, poor, and stagnant society.

British intellectuals in the 1600s had looked at India as very different from England, but not inferior. By 1800 these attitudes

The British who were stationed in India wished to change Indian society into a copy of life in Britain.

had changed. The nineteenth century was a time when many Europeans—especially the British—saw themselves as destined to be leaders of the world. The British regarded the native people they governed as children to be cared for and led. This was a duty; they called it the "white man's burden." Their aim was to transform Indian society into a copy of life in Britain.

Some of the practices in India shocked the moral attitudes of the British, particularly the Christian missionaries who had begun to take an interest in India. They were horrified by the tradition of *suttee*, an accepted custom among widows to burn themselves alive on their husbands' funeral pyres. Before long, laws were passed forbidding suttee.

Not everyone in England agreed about the proper role of the British in India. Lord Thomas Macaulay, a member of Parliament, held the revolutionary idea that India should be encouraged to progress toward independence and self-government. This could be accomplished, he believed, by giving the Indians an English education and by helping their economy to progress.

Lord Thomas Macaulay

The Sepoy Mutiny

Macaulay was a key figure in Parliament's Charter Act of 1833, a bill that ended the trade monopoly of the East India Company and opened the doors for British citizens to emigrate to India and do business there without restriction. The charter also forbade all discrimination in employment based on religion, descent, or color, and stated that the interests of native subjects (Indians) should take preference over Europeans in any dispute. These lofty ideals were never totally carried out, but at least they provided a legal model toward which to aim.

INDIA BECOMES PART OF THE EMPIRE

In 1857 about a third of the soldiers in the Indian army took part in a rebellion known in British history as the Sepoy Mutiny. The Indians call it their First War of Independence. Other small acts of rebellion were occurring at the same time in various parts of the country.

Complicated social and political changes were the underlying reasons for rebellion. There was widespread unemployment in the country, much of it because the British were no longer buying cotton cloth from India. The Industrial Revolution had brought factories to England, with machines that could turn out inexpensive textiles at home.

Laws passed by the British that infringed on the old customs were deeply resented by the Indians. The incidents of mutiny and rebellion added up to major revolt in 1857-58, and the British government took it seriously. The British Parliament decided that it was time to take India into the British Empire in a formal manner. All governing powers were taken away from the East India Company. A secretary of state for India was appointed, responsible directly to Parliament. The governor-general of India was named viceroy, the queen's personal representative.

Under the new regime, the British were careful not to upset Hindu or Muslim customs. Local princes were left alone, as long as they remained loyal to British supremacy. As it had been since the first merchants landed on the subcontinent, Britain's major aim was security and tranquility for carrying on trade.

Meanwhile, educated Indians were emerging who were eager to play a part in shaping the destiny of their country. A new sense of nationalism was developing. Indian representatives were included in legislative councils. In 1885 the Indian National Congress was founded.

William Gladstone, four times prime minister of Britain during the nineteenth century, once said about ruling India: "Good government is no substitute for self-government."

Swaraj, "self-rule," became the watchword for the twentieth century.

Chapter 7

THE LONG ROAD TO SWARAJ

Shortly after the British Empire took India under its wing in 1869, a baby was born in western India who was to become the most important person in India's modern history. Mohandas Karamchand Gandhi was the youngest member of an orthodox Hindu family of the merchant caste. His father was prime minister of the princely state of Porbandar.

Gandhi's mother's beliefs about nonviolence were close to those of the Jains, who were strong in that part of India. Like them, she was a strict vegetarian.

In the Hindu tradition, a marriage was arranged for Gandhi when he was thirteen years old. A few years later, with his mother's encouragement, he sailed for England to study law.

Gandhi became the greatest social reformer and political activist in India—perhaps in the entire world—but his work in India did not start until he was forty-six years old. After finishing his British education, he spent twenty-two years in South Africa working for the rights of Indians who live there.

In South Africa Gandhi learned how to organize masses of people to use nonviolent demonstrations as a way of protesting against repressive government actions. He was convinced that

A Bengal infantry division that served in Europe during World War I

ahimsa was a more effective weapon than violence in dealing with a powerful, well-armed enemy. He called his program of reform and nonviolent resistance *satyagraha*, which means "hold fast to the truth."

Returning to India during World War I, Gandhi was prepared to be a loyal citizen of the British Empire. He had been well educated and indoctrinated in English law and political theory, as had all of the other young Indian men who rose to positions of leadership under the British.

Even though some disturbances between the Indians and British had occurred from time to time during the previous few years, nearly every Indian prince and political leader was forced to give total support to Britain and its allies during the war. The first Indian Expeditionary Force included 16,000 British and 28,500 Indian troops. They were highly praised by a New York newspaper, the *World* with these words:

> What an army! Its "native" contingent belongs to a civilization that was old when Germany was a forest and early Britons stained their bodies blue.

Shortly after the war ended, cooperation between the British and Indian leaders disintegrated rapidly.

THE INDIAN NATIONAL CONGRESS

The Indian National Congress was formed in 1885 as a political club where the educated, middle-class Indians could meet and discuss their problems. Its membership included people from all over the country and from different religious groups and castes.

The British approved of the Congress at first. They regarded it as an unofficial advisory group that could keep the government in close communication with the people of India.

Before long, however, it became clear to members of the Congress that even if the British had good intentions, the system was not answering the needs of the people they governed. More and more, the Congress became a meeting ground for discussion of nationalism, self-government, and independence. As these ideas gained acceptance among the Indians, the Congress began to lose the approval of many of the British. Muslims had been members of the Congress from the start, but after a while they feared that the Hindu majority would not take enough interest in protecting minority rights. In 1906 the Muslim League was organized, with the purpose of working to improve the conditions of Muslims. The British realized they had not one, but two strong factions to contend with, neither of them happy with the British *raj* (rule).

AFTER WORLD WAR I

In 1917, before the war had ended, Parliament issued a formal declaration that self-government was the British objective for

India. Since this was exactly what the Indian leaders wanted also, it is hard to understand why it took another thirty years for the British to leave the country in the hands of its own people.

The truth is that most responsible leaders on both sides truly wanted the same thing: for India to become an independent nation with strong ties to Britain. The disagreement between them was over how quickly the transition to self-government should take place. And unfortunately, it seemed that too often one step forward was soon followed by two steps backward.

Instead of taking advantage of the strong spirit of cooperation, the British government passed legislation only a few months later that infuriated Indian leaders. New repressive laws gave judges the power to ignore the fundamental rights of citizens in the case of political uprisings. Secret trials before judges, without the right of counsel, jury, and appeal under the Rowlatt Acts of 1918, were an insult to the Indians and indicated to them that the British were not sincere about moving toward independence.

SATYAGRAHA

At this point Mohandas Gandhi emerged as a leader of the independence cause. He launched a program of political action unlike anything the world had ever seen. He declared that the Rowlatt Acts were symptoms "of a deep-seated disease in the governing body," and called for a nationwide boycott of all British institutions, including shops, universities, and government bodies.

Many Indian political leaders resigned their offices and turned back decorations they had received from the British government. Rabindranath Tagore, a world-famous writer and artist who had been knighted after receiving the Nobel Prize for literature in

Rabindranath Tagore

The young Mohandas K. Gandhi as barrister of law in London

1913, resigned his knighthood. Students stayed away from their university classes and people of all kinds picketed shops where British goods were sold. For the first time, there was nationwide action in India that cut across all divisions of language, region, and religion.

Public gatherings were banned. When ten thousand people, most of them peasants, came to Amritsar, Punjab, to celebrate a Hindu festival, Reginald Dyer, a British general, ordered his soldiers to fire on the crowd. After ten minutes, when over fifteen hundred rounds had been fired and the ammunition exhausted, Dyer marched his men out, leaving the dead and dying without attention. About four hundred Indians were killed and twelve hundred more were wounded. In Europe and America the Amritsar tragedy discredited the British occupation of India.

Gandhi was imprisoned in 1922 for civil disobedience, the first of many times. Over the years numerous other political activists were arrested frequently. It became a badge of honor to have served time for political reasons. In all, Gandhi spent about seven years of his life in prison.

Motilal Nehru (left), his son Jawaharlal Nehru (center), and Mahatma Gandhi (right)

GANDHI AND NEHRU

Among Gandhi's close friends and devoted followers were a wealthy father and son. Motilal Nehru was a well-educated lawyer who admired the British and had traveled to Europe several times. His son, Jawaharlal, who was to become India's first prime minister after independence, was raised in a luxurious home and educated in England, first at Harrow, an exclusive prep school, and then at Trinity College, Cambridge University.

Jawaharlal Nehru had become interested in the cause of Indian independence by the time Gandhi returned to India. Both of the Nehru men were very Westernized and aristocratic in their tastes, but they recognized that the small, modest man called *Gandhiji* by his followers had both the intelligence and the moral strength to lead the Indian people toward self-rule. The massacre in Amritsar was the incident that pushed both of them firmly into Gandhi's camp. Both Nehrus, like Gandhi, were arrested and imprisoned several times over the next few years.

Gandhi was dedicated to working for swaraj, but he did not blame all of India's troubles on the British. He wanted to see the British government leave, but he didn't think that would cure everything. Gandhi was a reformer. His program of reforms included many things he wanted to teach the Indians to do for themselves.

The *Mahatma* ("Great-Souled One"), as the Indian people began to call Gandhi, was especially interested in the plight of the untouchables, whom he called *harijans*, "children of God."

Gandhi was convinced that untouchability was a sin and that the Hindus themselves should take responsibility for outlawing the practice. Respect for all human beings was an important part of his philosophy of life. He wanted to achieve equality for women, and he wanted the rest of the world to accept Indians as equals.

While Gandhi always considered himself a Hindu, he believed that there are many roads leading to God. He had both Muslim and Christian friends, and he was thoroughly educated about these religions. He considered religion to be a personal matter that should not divide people who have a common cause.

Another part of Gandhi's belief was that life should be simple. If the villages could be self-sufficient, as they had been in earlier times, people would be happier. He urged Indians to rely on Indian handicrafts, *swadeshi* (literally, "of our own country"), in preference to imported goods. He wanted everyone—male and female, poor and rich—to do some hand spinning or weaving every day. This was a symbol, to him, of both self-discipline and self-sufficiency.

By the early 1920s, Gandhi had become the undisputed leader of the Indian National Congress. At first many Muslims followed his lead, but Muhammad Ali Jinnah, president of the Muslim League, was opposed to satyagraha. He represented the middle-class elite of the Muslims. While he, too, wanted to see India free, he feared that the Hindus, who were a large majority, would not protect the rights of Muslims. Gandhi tried repeatedly to gain Jinnah's cooperation and trust, but he never succeeded.

Jawaharlal Nehru was elected president of the Indian National Congress in 1929. He and Gandhi did not see eye to eye on everything. For example, Nehru did not really agree with Gandhi that small industries such as hand weaving and spinning were the answer to India's economic needs; he believed that heavy industry was needed as well. But their differences did not prevent the two men from being devoted friends, loyal to their mutual goal of independence for their country.

Gandhi sometimes felt that Nehru was too impatient for progress, but he wrote this about him when the younger man was elected:

> He is undoubtedly an extremist, thinking far
> ahead of his surroundings. But he is humble and
> practical enough not to force the pace to the
> breaking point. He is pure as crystal. He is
> truthful beyond suspicion . . . The nation is safe
> in his hands.

In 1930 Gandhi led his people in a protest somewhat like the Boston Tea Party that helped bring on the American Revolution. The manufacture and sale of salt was a British monopoly, and it was heavily taxed. It was illegal for any private party or company to make or sell salt; it was even illegal to gather natural sea salt.

Left: The Mahatma wore simple homespun clothing.
Above: Gandhi meets with Nehru just after Nehru had been elected president of the Indian National Congress.

The Mahatma decided to lead seventy-eight *satyagrahis* (followers of his nonviolent movement) on a 240-mile (386-kilometer) march to the seashore, where they would disobey the law by picking up natural salt. Gandhi was sixty-one years old and bald; he carried a walking stick and wore only a simple homespun cotton loincloth. At the end of the march he made a public statement that he had broken the law and called on other Indians to do so as well. He was arrested and spent eight months in prison.

This action was one of many over the years that resulted in strikes, protest marches, and imprisonment for tens of thousands of Gandhi's people.

The Indian people, for the most part, not only respected and trusted Gandhi as a political leader, they had great love for him as well. They called him by affectionate nicknames—Gandhiji and *Bapu* (father). Because of this close bond he had with millions of his countrymen and women, he was able to make use of another tactic to dramatize his causes. From time to time he would go on a fast, refusing to eat for days, or even weeks, at a time. The British were afraid to let him die, knowing how much this would upset the Indians, so these fasts were often a very effective means of political pressure.

Gandhi used fasting to teach lessons to the Indians, too. He would sometimes fast to persuade the Hindus and Muslims to stop rioting against each other. Once he fasted for three weeks as a protest against discriminatory practices toward the untouchables.

In 1935 Britain passed the Government of India Act, outlining a framework for self-government. It provided for elections that would expand the power of the states and provide special seats in a bicameral federal congress for minority groups—Muslims, untouchables, Anglo-Indians, and English people living in India. In the elections that followed, the Congress party won everywhere except in the areas with large Muslim populations—Assam, Bengal, and the area that is now Pakistan. The new act went into effect in 1937.

WORLD WAR II

Two years later World War II broke out in Europe. Britain automatically involved India in the conflict. Indian leaders were angry, and several Congress ministers resigned in protest. They were in complete sympathy with Britain's side in the war, but they resented bitterly the fact that they had not been consulted about the part their country would play. The Muslim League disagreed with the Congress party in this matter, and the split between the two groups grew wider than ever.

Gandhi started a movement to get the British out of India immediately. Violence flared up and relations between the British and the Hindus became bitter. The Muslim League became even more favored in the eyes of the British.

Gandhi and Jinnah met once more to try to end their stalemate, but without success. Gandhi wanted a united India that would include the Muslim areas; Jinnah was determined to hold out for a separate Pakistan.

At the end of the war, British people at home were tired, impoverished, and unable to hold onto India. They were unwilling to commit men or money to keeping peace in India, where riots were springing up and violent clashes were breaking out between Hindus and Muslims.

The British declared that August 15, 1947, would be India Independence Day and two new nations, India and Pakistan, would be self-governing dominions within the British Commonwealth of Nations on the same level with the Dominion of Canada.

The country celebrated independence with fireworks and parties, but bitter fighting continued between the Muslims and Hindus. Muslims living in India fled to Pakistan for refuge and Hindus in Pakistan left that new country to cross over into India.

Mahatma Gandhi was heartbroken over the failure of the two religious factions to get together under one united country. He began another fast in an effort to stop the rioting. Some fanatic Hindus believed he was too sympathetic to the Muslims. On

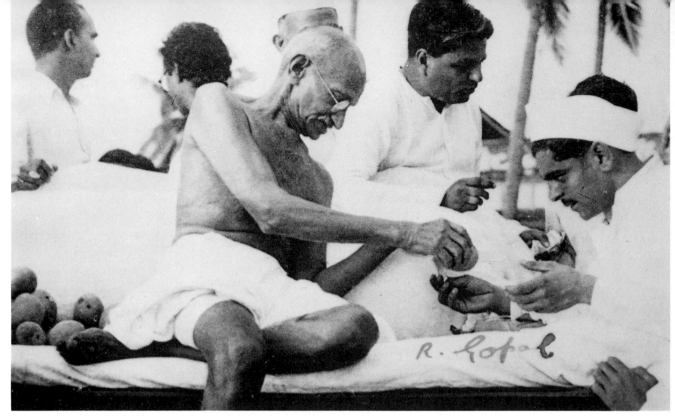

Gandhi distributing fruit after a prayer meeting (above). When Gandhi and his assistant, Miss Slade, traveled to Europe in the early 1930s, they were greeted by friends and reporters in Marseilles, France (below).

Visitors pay their respects at Mahatma Gandhi's memorial, Raj Ghat, in New Delhi.

January 30, 1948, less than six months after his goal of independence had been reached, the beloved leader was shot and killed while attending a prayer meeting in New Delhi. One of the bravest and most inspirational world leaders of the twentieth century fell at the hands of a terrorist.

Prime Minister Nehru mourned him with these words:

> A light has gone out of our lives and there is darkness everywhere . . . [yet] the light that shone . . . was no ordinary light. It will illuminate this country for many years, and a thousand years later it will be seen and it will give solace to innumerable hearts. For that represented something more than the immediate present, it represented the living truth, the eternal truth, reminding us of the right path . . . taking this ancient country to freedom.

Chapter 8

A NOISY AND DETERMINED DEMOCRACY

India's home rule became a reality in 1947, and Jawaharlal Nehru took office as the prime minister of the new member of the British Commonwealth. But the Indians were not satisfied with their status as a dominion, which implied that the country still owed a symbolic allegiance to the British crown. So on January 26, 1950, India adopted a new constitution and became the first republic in the Commonwealth.

Independence did not bring immediate solutions to India's many problems, such as poverty, overpopulation, and religious conflicts, of course. But her people have worked tirelessly to build a new nation firmly based on democratic principles.

Prime Minister Nehru led the government of India until his death in 1964. He was greatly respected all over the world.

Nehru believed strongly that India should follow a policy of nonalignment—that is, that it should remain friendly with all other nations, regardless of the powerful blocs that were then choosing up sides behind the leadership of the United States and the Soviet Union. He called his concept *panchsheel*, and defined it as "respect for territorial integrity and sovereignty, non-aggression, non-interference in others' internal affairs, equality and peaceful co-existence."

Nehru, as prime minister of India, addresses a crowd.

Despite the sincere desire of Nehru and other Indian leaders to live peacefully with the rest of the world, relations with Pakistan were not good. But Nehru told his people that their real enemies were not the people of other nations, but poverty, corruption, laziness, and inefficiency, and that these evils must be conquered before independence would have true meaning.

Under his leadership, a series of Five-Year Plans for economic development were set in motion. New steel plants, oil refineries, and hydroelectric complexes were built, and modernization of farming methods was encouraged. Nehru believed in preserving the best of the country's cultural heritage, but he also believed in using modern technology and science to improve the nation's standard of living.

Nehru also worked to improve the status of Indian women. He eliminated sex discrimination in government employment and

Left: Indira Gandhi with her father Jawaharlal Nehru
Right: Mrs. Gandhi with her two sons, Rajiv (left) and Sanjay (right)

encouraged women to become educated and to participate in
political leadership.

Peace among nations was a major goal for the prime minister
and he was heartbroken when fighting along the Indian-Chinese
border broke out briefly in 1962.

In 1964 the great leader suffered a stroke and he died a few
weeks later, in May. The second of the two giants who had led the
country to independence was gone.

SINCE NEHRU

Nehru's descendants have dominated India's political scene
most of the time since his death. His daughter, Mrs. Indira Gandhi
(not related to the Mahatma), was named prime minister in 1966
and served until 1977, when her party lost its power in Congress.
She regained the office in 1980.

Old problems between India and Pakistan resulted in an outbreak of fighting in 1971. As a result of that war, Pakistan lost control of the eastern part of her territories, which became the new nation of Bangladesh.

In October 1984 Indira Gandhi was assassinated by one of her own personal bodyguards, a member of a group of extremist Sikhs. Her son Rajiv Gandhi was named her successor.

After parliamentary elections in 1989, Rajiv Gandhi resigned and Vishwanath Pratap Singh became prime minister.

GOVERNMENT

India's constitution declares it to be a "sovereign socialist secular democratic republic."

The constitution of the Republic of India protects the fundamental rights of all citizens, such as freedom of speech, assembly, and religion. It also provides for free choice of occupation or trade and for protection against discrimination on the grounds of race, religion, creed, or sex. These provisions, as they become more widely accepted and enforced, will gradually break down ancient restrictions based on caste.

India is a parliamentary democracy. The national government has three branches: the executive, judicial, and legislative (Parliament). Local government is administered by twenty-five states and seven union territories.

All natives of India who are twenty-one years of age or older are citizens with the right to vote, unless they are disqualified on grounds of mental illness or criminal involvement. There are no requirements for literacy. Ballots are printed with picture symbols representing different political parties, along with printed words

*The peacock (left), India's national bird,
and the Lion Capital of Asoka (right)*

and names. This gives a choice to all voters, even those who cannot read. More than half the eligible voters turn out for elections.

NATIONAL SYMBOLS

The Indian flag has three broad horizontal stripes of saffron, white, and green. Saffron is the sacred color of Hinduism and green is the color of Islam. The official interpretation of the significance of these colors in the flag is: saffron for courage and sacrifice, white for truth and peace, and green for faith and chivalry.

In the center of the white stripe is a navy-blue wheel, called the *chakra*, a form found in ancient Indian art standing for the law of dharma. A wheel also stands for movement, or progress. In addition, the wheel recalled the *charkha* (spinning wheel), used by Gandhi as a symbol of independence and a part of the flag of the Indian National Congress.

The official emblem is an adaptation of a museum piece known as the Lion Capital of Asoka. (Capital, in this context, means the top of an architectural column or pillar.) The capital is a block of polished sandstone sculpted with four lions standing back to back on an ornamental pedestal decorated with animals, charkhas, and a lotus. The state emblem carries the words *Satyameva jayate* in Sanskrit, which means "Truth alone triumphs."

The peacock is India's national bird, a favorite with the Indian people for centuries. Many superstitions and folktales about peacocks have been told for generations. Its brilliant plumage makes it an appropriate symbol for this colorful country.

FOREIGN POLICY

India has continued to follow Nehru's policy of nonalignment in an attempt to stay friendly with all the major powers of the world. More than one hundred of the world's countries, representing nearly two-thirds of all the people on earth, have joined with India in declaring themselves to be "nonaligned."

Independent India takes a leadership role within the United Nations against colonialism or racism in other nations. Wherever possible, India gives economic and technical assistance to other developing countries.

THE RAJAHS

When the British ruled India, they actually had direct control over only about three-fourths of the country's area. The rest was divided into 554 separate tiny princedoms ruled by rajahs who had signed agreements with the British. These rajahs were given the choice of declaring their areas independent countries or joining with one of the new nations, India or Pakistan.

Actually, they had little choice, since a tiny nation surrounded by a huge one would not be able to be very independent. So they merged, and in India they were permitted to retain their titles and were granted huge incomes from the national government to make up for what they had lost.

Since India's independence, many people have come to resent any special privileges given to the rajahs, and the titles have become less meaningful. Though many still hold a certain amount of political power, most young descendants of Indian princes who once were among the world's richest people have had to make new lives for themselves in business or professions.

INDUSTRY

Textile manufacturing is India's most important industry, just as it has been since the days when the European traders first came to the shores of the Indian Ocean.

Heavy industries and electronics are gaining steadily in importance. Modern plants turn out steel, machinery, engineering goods, and chemicals. Huge pipelines carry oil and gas from offshore fields near Bombay to other parts of the country. Six nuclear reactors generate electric power.

Industrial progress sometimes brings disastrous consequences, however. A great tragedy occurred in the city of Bhopal, India, in December 1984. A deadly gas leak from tanks owned and operated by the Union Carbide Company of the United States caused more than twenty-five hundred deaths. This was the worst industrial accident in the history of the world.

*Some of India's diverse industry,
clockwise from bottom left:
steel mills at Burnpur Asansol,
manufacturing rims for motorcycles,
and textile factory workers
spreading dyed fabric to dry*

Research and development programs in the fields of aerospace
technology, computers, oceanography, and biotechnology are all
assisted as a part of the nation's seventh Five-Year Plan.

At the same time, ancient Indian handicrafts are not neglected.
Hand-knotted wool and silk carpets, art metalware, hand-loomed
and hand-printed fabrics, and handmade goods of leather, wood,
and cane are exported all over the world. The production of
handicrafts is an important means of employment for millions of
village workers.

AGRICULTURE

About 70 percent of India's people depend on farming for a
living. While many of them are very poor, barely managing to
survive, improved agricultural methods have brought about a
great increase in production during the end of the twentieth

Testing river water for signs of pollution

century. The amount of land under irrigation has more than doubled since 1950. Careful use of fertilizers and pesticides has been helpful. The government is keenly aware of environmental issues, and care is taken to avoid short-term measures that would harm the total ecological system of the country. Wheat, rice, cotton, and jute are major agricultural products.

Active government programs are underway to bring electricity and safe drinking water to all the villages.

TRANSPORTATION

India's railroad system is one of the most extensive and most widely used in the world. It has been in place for so long that it seems almost to be a part of the ancient Indian civilization. Indian tradition and family duties demand that family members who have left home must make frequent visits to celebrate important occasions. Without the railroad, these duties could not be fulfilled. Fares are kept low in order to serve as many people as possible.

People boarding a crowded train (left) and a sign in Bombay showing some unusual traffic restrictions

By many measures, the Indian railway system could be called the greatest in the world—it has the most trains, the most stations, and carries the most passengers. Improvements in service, cleanliness, and general efficiency are badly needed, but without the railroad India would find it almost impossible to function.

Air traffic in India is served by several international and eighty domestic airports. Helicopter service is available to remote parts of the Himalaya and certain islands.

India's highway system has been enlarged and improved in recent years. The mixture of old and new India is most apparent and colorful on her roadways. All kinds of vehicles crowd the routes, most of them made in India—cars, jeeps, trucks, vans, buses, and a variety of two-wheeled motorbikes. They weave in and out of traffic and rush past carts and wagons drawn by bullocks, horses, and camels.

Chapter 9

A COLORFUL DIVERSITY

Color, color, everywhere. A first-time visitor to India is fascinated by the brilliant colors. Women's *saris* might be noticed first. To make a sari, one end of a long piece of cloth is wrapped around the body to form a skirt and the other end becomes a shoulder or head covering. A matching or coordinated blouse or sweater is worn with it. Wealthy women own dozens of saris. A bride's family may help her gather a trousseau of one hundred saris. Every vivid shade is used—scarlet, fiery orange, iridescent pinks, blues, greens, and aquamarines. Gold and silver threads are woven into the silk fabric. Poorer women in the villages may possess only a few saris, and they probably are made of cotton instead of silk, but the colors are just as bright and cheerful.

There are many different ways to wear a sari. Women from Rajasthan wear a very wide cotton skirt, and those from the eastern part of the country have narrow skirts.

Punjabi women wear a long overblouse and loose pants gathered at the ankles. Some Muslim women cover themselves in a large hooded cape that shows nothing but their eyes.

In the cities most men wear Western suits, but in the country their clothing and the way they drape their turbans signifies their home area.

Opposite page: The brilliant colors of India

Above: Most women have their noses as well as their ears pierced.
Right: Delicate mosaic decorations on the City Palace in Jaipur

JEWELRY

Indian jewelry is intricately fashioned of gold, precious stones, enamel, and glass. Women wear many rings, necklaces, hair ornaments, and anklets. Their arms are covered with bangles (bracelets) made of gold, silver, or glass. Nearly every female, child or adult, has her nose pierced as well as her ears, and wears tiny sparkling gems in her nose and ears.

A Hindu woman wears a round spot of powder on her forehead, red or a color that matches her sari. This may have had a religious significance once, but today it is merely cosmetic.

Ancient buildings are colorful, too—made of red sandstone or decorated with mosaics of tile and brilliant gems. Temples, some

Huge, colorful posters advertise movies, which are very popular in India.

of them hundreds of years old, are decorated with bright murals that illustrate ancient tales in fine detail.

In the cities huge hand-painted posters, also in brilliant colors, are used to advertise movies and commercial products. One could live for a year in each of the nation's thirty-two states and territories and still not have visited all the villages, celebrated all the festivals, or studied all the ancient customs.

The country has so many people who speak different languages, dress differently, eat different foods, and live different life-styles, that it is difficult for an outsider to believe this is a single nation.

Yet this is one of the world's oldest civilizations. It has existed for almost five thousand years, and in spite of repeated invasions by foreigners, India's own unique culture has survived.

Village houses in Rajasthan and the cool, pleasant interior of one of them

FAMILY LIFE

The glue that has held this civilization together through the ages is the closeness of Indian family life. It is traditional for extended families to live together, especially in the villages. Grandparents, uncles, aunts, and cousins are all part of the family. The land and home, or homes, are owned jointly by all of them. Wages are pooled.

When a son marries, he brings his bride into his parents' home. All the adult women take responsibility for household duties and caring for all the children. Toys are shared and children of all ages play together. Meals are generally served in three shifts—children first, then the men, and finally the women.

Village houses are commonly made of mud reinforced with straw. There is no glass in the small window openings. The walls are thick and ceilings are high, to keep out the heat of the summer, the monsoon rains, and the winter's cold. One room may be set aside to house a few farm animals. All the others are used as bedrooms at night and as places to sit during the day—when anyone is indoors. But most daily activities take place outside, on a veranda or in a courtyard.

Many village houses have electricity but no running water. Most villages are now being supplied with safe drinking water from village well pumps. Bathing is done in lakes, streams, or near wells. Women carry water to their homes from a stream or, more often, from a village pump. The government is making great strides toward providing both electricity and safe drinking water to every village.

MARRIAGE AND THE STATUS OF WOMEN

Marriages are usually arranged for young people by the older members of the family. Because of the closeness of the extended family, it is taken for granted that this arrangement is better than the Western custom of choosing one's own mate. Young people believe their parents will choose wisely for them, and that husband and wife will learn to love each other after marriage. And the custom does result, usually, in bringing together two people who have much in common: similar backgrounds, standards of living, traditions, and beliefs.

The selection often is made when the couple are both very young. At one time marriages took place between children, although the bride did not move into her husband's home until she was older. Today girls must be at least fifteen and boys eighteen for a legal Hindu marriage.

Hindu weddings are as elaborate as the family can afford. Huge

A bride and groom

parties and feasts are given, and all the relatives are expected to attend. Red is the traditional color for the bride's wedding sari. The wedding ceremony concludes when a Hindu priest ties the end of the bride's sari to the groom's scarf, after which the two of them walk together, seven times, around a fire.

After marriage a Hindu wife devotes most of her time to raising children and taking care of the family, which includes waiting on her husband. Many modern, well-educated women have distinguished careers of their own, but they still are expected to heed their husband's wishes. Divorce is allowed in India today, but it is a very rare occurrence.

EDUCATION

Most children of wealthy families attend private day schools or boarding schools, where rules are strict and the curriculum is geared to preparation for a university education. Students dress in school uniforms and are given courses in the arts and sports as well as academics.

High school students during student government elections (left) and on break between classes (right)

Village children, on the other hand, attend school irregularly or in some cases not at all. Many reasons keep them away from class. Their parents need their help in the fields or to care for a younger brother or sister. Village schools are simple. Pupils sit on a dirt floor in a small room or under a tree outofdoors. Books and other materials are scarce. Many Indian states have village school lunch programs to improve the nutrition of the children.

The national government has given a high priority to improving the level of education in India. A program of action authorized by Parliament in 1986 set up a national system of education whose goal is to provide free and compulsory education by 1995 for all children up to the age of fourteen.

CITY HOMES

Middle-class city dwellers live in small apartments or modest brick homes. Floors are made of cement or terrazzo, the windows have glass panes, and there are bathrooms with toilets, sinks, and showers—but in apartment houses more than one family may share a bathroom.

Right: Many Indians are able to live a comfortable life. However, a large number of Indians are poor and homeless and live in the streets (below). Mother Teresa (below right) has dedicated her life to helping India's poor.

Furniture in a typical home consists of a table, a few chairs, and a cot for sleeping. Women do their cooking on gas stoves in urban areas, either in a squatting or sitting position.

Many people in India's huge cities are poor and homeless. The homeless live and sleep on the city streets, and some find employment as hawkers or manual laborers.

Widespread poverty is India's greatest problem, and everyone, both the Indian people and foreigners who visit the country, would like to see conditions improved.

A woman who has made a life work ministering to Calcutta's poor people is a Roman Catholic nun originally from Yugoslavia. Mother Teresa, called affectionately the "saint of the gutter," is one of India's most internationally known citizens. She was awarded the Nobel Peace Prize in 1979 for her widespread services in founding hospitals, schools, orphanages, and shelters for lepers and other needy people.

A Republic Day parade in New Delhi (above), and a young man decorating his bullock for a village festival (left)

FESTIVALS

Religious and secular customs blend together in India, especially when it comes to celebrations. So many different festivals are observed in different parts of the country that one could probably find one somewhere on nearly every day of the year. Many different Hindu deities are honored on their own special day or season. Each temple has an annual festival dedicated to its own particular god or goddess. Changes of seasons are welcomed with festivals. Many celebrations are held in the autumn to honor the harvest. A festival of lights ushers in the winter with fireworks, gifts, and games. Tribal festivals are unique to particular regions.

Festivals are a time for families and friends to come together for feasting and observing certain rituals. Processions, fairs, and street entertainment are a part of the celebrations. Uniformed soldiers, richly garbed nobles, and elephants in glittering attire march to the sound of trumpets and drums.

The festival of Holi, in March, is observed all over the country with music and dance. People wear old clothes and throw tinted powder or colored water on each other.

Muslims, Christians, Jains, and Parsis celebrate their religious holidays with as much devotion but considerably less color and pageantry than the Hindus. Christmas is celebrated by both Christians and non-Christians.

January 26 is Republic Day, which commemorates India becoming the first republic in the Commonwealth and the adoption of the constitution. It is marked by parades and pageants. August 15 is celebrated as Independence Day.

Mahatma Gandhi's birthday, October 2, is a day of remembrance, and Jawaharlal Nehru's birthday, November 14, is celebrated throughout the country as Children's Day.

FOOD

As in every other aspect of everyday life, there is great variety in the diet of different Indians. Jains, with their attitude toward the sanctity of all living creatures, do not eat meat. Neither do many Hindus and Buddhists. Muslims do eat meat, but not pork. Hindus who do eat some meats will not eat beef, as cows are considered sacred. Even vegetarians have certain taboos against some vegetables or some methods of cooking.

Because of these differences, most Indian dinner parties are served in both vegetarian and non-vegetarian buffet style, so that guests can eat according to their individual preferences.

Flat cakes made of wheat flour, called *chappatis* or *rotis*, are a

Left and above left: Some snacks that street vendors sell.
Above: Succulent beef curry and a plate of poppadoms—
individual flat breads.

staple for most Indians, as are rice, curries, and yogurt. Indians
drink milk from buffaloes, cows, and goats. It is proper to eat with
the tips of one's fingers, but only with the right hand. Chappatis
and rice rolled into little balls are used to pick up the curries.

Western cooks ordinarily buy prepared curry powder, but
Indian housewives mix their own from fresh spices, typically
coriander, mustard, tumeric, garlic, onions, and anise seeds.
Vegetables and meats are cooked with curry.

Many different kinds of fruits and nuts are plentiful in some
parts of India. Coconut milk is a popular refreshing drink and tea
and coffee are popular too.

COMPLEX AND FASCINATING

India is so large, so complex, and so fascinating, it is hard for a
visitor to choose among its many historic and scenic areas. But

three cities stand out as the first places most foreigners want to see: Delhi, Agra, and Jaipur. They are the points of a triangle with only about 100 miles (161 kilometers) on each side. Decent highways make travel between these points easy.

DELHI

Delhi has been an urban settlement for at least fifteen centuries, according to archaeological evidence. Legends, on the other hand, tell of the city of Indraprastha, which may have been on this site as early as three thousand years ago. New towns have been built here, adjacent to the ruins of older ones, time and time again. Historians and archaeologists speak of seven different medieval cities. Later Mughals and then the British added structures.

Today New Delhi is the capital and third-largest city of modern India. New hotels, office buildings, and apartment complexes have risen amid the ancient forts and temples. Traders and artisans hawk their wares in open-air markets, against a backdrop of Oriental spires, minarets, and marble domes.

More than thirteen hundred monuments and ruins in Delhi are on official historic lists. One of the most imposing is the Red Fort, or Lal Qila. This fortified sandstone palace was built by Shah Jahan, the Mughal emperor who created the famous Taj Mahal. He planned a city around the complex and named it Shahjahanabad, after his own name. Lal Qila was a splendid complex containing a copper-domed mosque, marble buildings, gardens, and running streams. Sound-and-light shows that relate the history of the fort are presented each evening except during rainy seasons.

Humayun's Tomb, a forerunner of the Taj Mahal, is a mixture

*Scenes of Delhi clockwise
from top left: Humayun's Tomb,
the India Gate, and a complex
of new apartment buildings*

of Persian and Indian architectural styles, a tomb within a garden,
built of red sandstone and black and white marble. Many of the
Mughal nobility were buried here.

New Delhi was built by the British on a site south of
Shahjahanabad. Two architects were given the job of designing a
new capital for British India. It was inaugurated in 1931.
Parliament House, the India Gate (a memorial to the ninety
thousand Indian soldiers who died in World War I), and the 340-
room presidential palace are among the structures.

Raj Ghat, the Gandhi Shrine, is a simple memorial to the
humble man who did so much for India. It is a stone-enclosed
space with a black marble platform in the center, marking the spot
of the Mahatma's cremation. Visitors remove their shoes before

Shops and traffic in the central business district of New Delhi (left) and the crowded Chandni Chowk shopping area (right) in Old Delhi

walking into the garden area. A small museum nearby contains mementos of Gandhi's life.

The Nehru Memorial Museum, where India's first prime minister lived for the last sixteen years of his life, is now a museum. The many photographs, letters, and personal possessions on display give visitors an insight into the life of this remarkable man.

At the south edge of the city is the Baha'i House of Worship, completed in 1986. It is a most unusual modern structure, in the shape of a lotus blossom. Spacious landscaped grounds surround the marble-clad building.

AGRA

Without a doubt, Agra's Taj Mahal is India's most famous landmark. The symmetry of its shape and the serene reflecting pool in front of it are well known all over the world, through

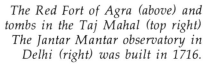
The Red Fort of Agra (above) and
tombs in the Taj Mahal (top right)
The Jantar Mantar observatory in
Delhi (right) was built in 1716.

pictures. What astonishes the person who has the opportunity to
actually approach and walk inside it, is the incredible, intricate
delicacy of the mosaic work. The marble tile walls of the
mausoleum are adorned with inlays of semiprecious and precious
stones set in the shapes of graceful flowers. Although the
structure is lovely from a distance, the artistry of the inlay work
only can be appreciated at close hand.

Twenty thousand workers were involved in building the Taj,
which was completed in 1653.

Two other major points of interest in Agra are another tomb
decorated with inlaid marble, the Itimad-ud-Daula and the Red
Fort.

Agra's Red Fort is about seventy-five years older than the one in
Delhi. Its outer wall is nearly 2 miles (3.2 kilometers) long. Many
of the impressive buildings within the fort were built during the
rule of Shah Jahan, obviously a man of great architectural genius.

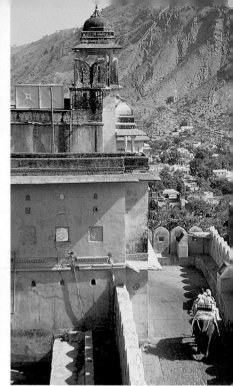

The Palace of Winds (left) and the main gate of the Amber Palace (right)

JAIPUR

Jaipur, called the "pink city," is the capital of the state of Rajasthan. In 1883 the ruling maharaja ordered its buildings, originally light gray, to be painted pink, the traditional color of welcome in India. The redecorating was done to honor the visit of Prince Albert, Queen Victoria's husband.

The City Palace, part of which is still used as a residence and part is open to the public as a museum, is a treasure house of textiles, carpets, and art objects that demonstrate the luxurious life-style enjoyed by the maharajas. The Jantar Mantar, a magnificent and modern-looking observatory with sun dial, was built in 1716.

Several imposing forts stand on the hills around Jaipur. Visitors can take an elephant ride up the hill to the fort at Amber. Two former palaces in the Jaipur area have been converted into hotels, where visitors can fantasize about the life of the maharajas and their families.

Farmers in small boats (right) sell produce and flowers to people living in the houseboats (left) on Dal Lake.

NORTH

The Kashmir valley has few equals in the world for unforgettable natural beauty. Its floor of deep green rice fields is dotted here and there by orchards and striped with lines of tall trees. Surrounding it are the great snow-capped peaks of the Himalaya.

Kashmir's handicrafts are some of the finest in India. Soft woolen shawls, appliqued felt rugs, enameled papier-mâché boxes and other articles, and hand-carved walnut furniture are among prized Kashmir products.

Most visitors to Kashmir try to spend some time on a houseboat on Dal Lake, at Srinagar. Houseboats here are used as floating hotels. Farmers sail among the larger vessels in little skiffs, selling vegetables and flowers. The city is worth visiting for its outstanding gardens and wonderfully decorated mosques.

Left: Bathing in the holy Ganges River   Right: The old section of Varanasi

Srinagar is a takeoff point for treks across the Kashmir valley and for mountain climbing and skiing in the Himalaya.

EAST

Varanasi, formerly called Benares, is Hinduism's holiest city. Thousands of Hindus make a pilgrimage here in order to visit its temples and bathe in the holy Ganges River. Five miles (eight kilometers) north of Varanasi, in the little town of Sarnath, is an impressive Buddhist temple, and in a museum across the street from the temple is the glazed Lion Capital, a piece of sculpture that has been adopted as India's national symbol.

Farther east is Darjeeling, just south of the state of Sikkim. It is a delightful mountain resort town on the slopes of the Himalaya. It is famous for a species of tea that has been exported around the world. Many Tibetan refugees live here and in Sikkim.

Top left: Picking tea on the steep slopes of Darjeeling
Top right: The Ghoom Buddhist Monastery in Darjeeling
Left: Calcutta has enormous problems with poverty and slums.

Mountain peaks in Sikkim are the highest in the nation. Sikkim was an independent kingdom until 1975, when the monarchy was abolished. It borders on Tibet and Nepal, and its population is largely Buddhist. There are several interesting Buddhist monasteries to visit.

Calcutta is India's largest city, with more than ten million people, and one of the world's most crowded. It is a city of bewildering contrasts, from peaceful gardens to teeming outdoor markets, stately homes to communities of street people.

Left: Street scene in Calcutta   Right: Street vendors in Madras

Something is always going on in this city—religious celebrations, festivals, political demonstrations, or athletic contests.

SOUTH

Madras, the nation's fourth-largest city, is the gateway to South India. The pace here is much more relaxed than in the cities to the north. Rivers and canals cross the city, with gardens alongside. The climate is tropical; there are palm trees and beaches. Fort St. George was constructed by the British East India Company; a museum within it has an interesting collection of items from the early days of the company.

Christian influence in Madras was greater than in many other parts of the country; St. George's Cathedral and St. Andrew's Kirk are two landmarks dating from the nineteenth century. Two important Hindu temples are Kapaleswara Shiva Temple, part of a

Top: The Victoria Memorial in Calcutta is a museum. Above: A quaint bullock cart on the street in Madras makes the ever-present movie posters seem even more garish. Left: In Madras, laundry washed in a river is spread out to dry.

complex called Mylapore, and Krishna Parathasarathy Temple. The arts are important in this city; there are fine museums, galleries, and theaters.

Tours of ancient Hindu temples with some outstanding examples of early architecture and sculpture go out from Madras to the small towns of Kanchipuram and Mamallapuram. The route lies close to the sandy beaches and the sea.

The state of Kerala is a narrow strip along the southwestern tip of India. Its population is very diverse, with Hindus, Muslims, Christians, and Jews who represent many different castes and sects. This fertile, lush region is the land of spices Christopher Columbus was looking for. It has towering coconut palm trees, fine old residences, and highly decorated, stunning palaces.

Left: A Portuguese church in Goa decorated for a festival Right: The Gateway to India in Bombay was built in 1911 to commemorate the visit of British King George V.

WEST

Goa, the newest and tiniest of India's twenty-five states, is very different from other parts of the nation. Portuguese traders landed here in 1510, and for the next 450 years it, along with two neighboring districts, was a Portuguese colony. Its 65-mile (105-kilometer) coastline and the architecture of the coastal towns remind visitors of Mediterranean shores. Gothic and Renaissance-style churches are evidence of the Catholic heritage brought by the Portuguese. Old Goa has many splendid churches and other buildings erected during the sixteenth century. Later Hindu temples can be found in the outskirts of the city, their architecture showing elements of Islamic and Christian styles.

Bombay is India's second most populous city and busiest port. Its fine natural harbor has made it the country's most important commercial and industrial center. Some people claim that it is the best place in India to buy native merchandise.

Bombay is a melting pot of many religions and language groups. During the late nineteenth century, the city prospered from a boom in cotton exporting. Many impressive British colonial buildings date from that period. There are no ancient or medieval landmarks within the city, but on an island in the harbor, about six miles (ten kilometers) from shore, there is a

Scenes of Bombay clockwise from top left: Victoria Station in the central business district, Marine Drive, Victoria Gardens surrounding the Victoria and Albert Museum, and a fishing boat in the harbor

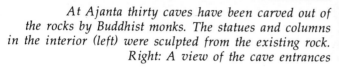

*At Ajanta thirty caves have been carved out of
the rocks by Buddhist monks. The statues and columns
in the interior (left) were sculpted from the existing rock.
Right: A view of the cave entrances*

series of cave temples, with huge Buddhist sculptures cut in the
rock. They were sculpted some twelve hundred years ago.

Other, even more impressive, Buddhist cave temples are found a
few hundred miles inland from Bombay, in Ellora and Ajanta.

ANIMALS IN INDIA

Everywhere in rural India there is a great deal of animal life,
both domesticated and wild. Camels, buffaloes, horses, bullocks,
and goats are used to pull carts and wagons. Ducks, geese, and
chickens are raised for food.

Cows are considered to be sacred in India because their milk is
symbolic of the spirit of divine motherhood, comfort, and
nurturing.

Monkeys are regarded with special affection and Hanuman, the
monkey king, is a favorite figure in Hindu religious tales.

Above: Indians have a special affection for monkeys.
Left: Project Tiger is dedicated to the preservation
of the Bengal tiger.

The ancient Indian tradition of respect for all forms of life is expressed today in the setting aside of wilderness areas. The government has created 247 wildlife sanctuaries and 53 national parks, where tigers, bears, elephants, monkeys, yaks, wild buffaloes, rhinos, panthers, and countless smaller animals and birds are protected. Project Tiger, launched under the direction of Prime Minister Indira Gandhi in 1973, is an ambitious program dedicated to the preservation of India's magnificent tigers and the environment they live in.

INDIA'S WILDLIFE

It is difficult for a country with a rapidly expanding population to set aside land for the preservation of wildlife, but India's national policy is to save its rich natural heritage. Approximately three hundred wildlife sanctuaries and national parks occupy about 3 percent of the nation's land area and 12 percent of the total forest area. Visitors can go to these sanctuaries and, if they are lucky, spot many species of animals and birds, some of them very rare, in their native habitat.

Indians decorate their elephants as well as themselves. The man at upper left has painted himself as a tiger for a Hindu festival. Left: An elderly gentleman dying material for saris

Chapter 10

THE ARTS
AND ENTERTAINMENT

Indians have a love of ornamentation unequaled in the world. Their love of beauty finds expression in every imaginable form—paintings, textiles, jewelry, decorated boxes, embroidery, and much more. Intricate details and elaborate patterns, along with brilliant colors, are used in hundreds of ways.

Different colors are said to have distinct meanings and to evoke distinct emotions. Red is the color of love. Orange is the earth. Yellow reminds one of spring. Blue is the color of the god Krishna and is related to clouds and rain.

From the days when the first sailing vessels brought the first foreign merchants to India's shores, artisans have been making ornamental objects for sale to the rest of the world. But not all handicrafts are created for the marketplace; many objects made for personal, everyday use are equally decorative. In some remote hill villages, every household utensil and every piece of clothing is as brightly and elaborately embellished as goods made for sale to tourists.

One village in northwest India, called Bhujodi, is known for the beautiful relief work that decorates the inside walls of the homes. Peacocks and parrots, elephants and camels, trees and plants, are featured along with geometric designs, tiny mirrors, and a

Close-ups of the henna decorations with which many young brides adorn their hands and feet

representation of Kanudo (the young god Krishna). All this artistic expression is the work of untrained artisans, working with the mixture of mud and animal dung that is the common local building material. When the material is dry, the walls are whitewashed.

People decorate themselves as well as their surroundings. Many young brides have *mehndi* paste applied to their hands and feet. This is an application of henna dye, painted on in patterns that look like the finest lace gloves and stockings.

RELIGION AND THE ARTS

Just as many everyday customs in India are rooted in religion, so are its traditional literature, poetry, paintings, sculpture, dance, and drama. Even today many Indian temples have their own resident craftspeople—sculptors, painters, weavers, and other artisans.

A musician playing a sitar (left), and dancers performing a traditional monkey dance

The basis for all the arts is the great body of Vedic literature. The two great Sanskrit epics, the *Mahabharata* and the *Ramayana*, were told orally from generation to generation before they were written down. They were performed in Hindu temples by dancers wearing elaborate costumes and masks or heavy makeup.

Classical dances are still performed today, and many parts of the country also have their own regional folk dances.

PAINTINGS

Traditional paintings tell a story. They are not merely to be looked at, but to be read also. Many of the most splendid ones were introduced to India during the Mughal period and reflect the Islamic tradition. People in the paintings are usually dressed in elaborate costumes, embroidered and encrusted with jewels and gold thread. Each tiny gem can be seen. The pictured walls are

The intricate and splendid decorations of Indian architecture can be seen in the temple ruins at Hampi (left) and the Peacock Gate of City Palace (right) in Jaipur.

carved, carpets are patterned, each leaf and blade of grass stands on its own. There are paintings on silk, ivory, paper, cotton, and palm leaves. The oldest known Indian paintings are Buddhist frescoes in Ajanta.

Modern versions of traditional story paintings can be seen in Bengal villages, where a local folk artist, called *patua*, tells stories through pictures painted on scrolls of paper. The patua sings or chants the story as he unfolds the painting. Some of the picture tales are ancient stories, some are taken from contemporary events.

SCULPTURE AND ARCHITECTURE

Early Indian sculptors made figures of gods and goddesses in stone, and later in terra-cotta. They were fanciful figures, some of them part animal, others with many arms. The art took on more human form around the first century A.D.

The Mughal period was one of decline for sculpture, as the Muslims considered it to be the creation of idols. But the Mughals encouraged the arts of literature, calligraphy, and book illustration.

Emperor Akbar was illiterate and not interested in literature; he encouraged the art of painting. Paintings of this period became more realistic and depicted ordinary people as well as aristocracy.

Architecture, too, flourished under the Mughals, and the supreme example is the Taj Mahal. Buildings of ancient India were decorated with carvings, stone filigree, arches, and cupolas. Artisans in Agra carry on the art, making tabletops, trays, boxes, and tiles of marble and gemstones like those used for the walls of the Taj.

TEXTILES

Indian textiles—cotton, silk, and wool—woven, hand painted, or embroidered in brilliant colors and intricate designs have been known and prized throughout the world for centuries. Textiles fashioned by Indian master weavers were worn by emperors of ancient Rome, China, and Byzantium.

Today's weavers can reproduce the rich brocades of the past; they also continue to create new patterns. It is claimed that if a single flaw is found in a tapestry made for a Hindu temple, the entire bolt of cloth is destroyed. Cloths from India are used in Mecca's holiest Islamic places and are made into vestments worn by the pope.

Some twenty-four million Indians are employed in the textile industry. Weaving is traditionally done by men, embroidery by women.

Rugs woven and tied by hand, of wool and silk, are equally fine.

*Among the highly prized crafts of India
are hand-painted fabric (above),
marble inlaid tables (above right),
and hand-woven rugs (right)*

HANDICRAFTS

Different regions of the country specialize in different crafts. Some of the finest come from Kashmir—objects made of papier-mâché, crewel embroidery, carved ivories, silverware, carpets, and shawls. Kashmiri arts display the colors and shapes of the beautiful Kashmiri landscape and the region's flora and fauna.

Rajasthan and Uttar Pradesh are famous for metalwork—bowls, boxes, vases, and ornaments fashioned of brass, copper, silver, and gold and hammered into shape, engraved, or enameled in bright colors.

Even though furniture is sparsely used in Indian homes, as it is in many other countries, the country has fine cabinetmakers. They turn out chairs, sofas, lamps, and bedsteads that are carved and shaped into objects of art. Trunks and chests are inlaid with ivory, mother-of-pearl, tortoise shell, and gems.

Above left: A game of volleyball
Left: An artist engraving a brass vessel
Above: A crowd waiting to be admitted to a movie

ENTERTAINMENT

By far the most popular form of entertainment in India is the movies. The film industry in India produces more movies annually than any other country—more than eight hundred full-length features a year, plus numerous documentaries and short features.

The major moviemaking centers are Bombay, Madras, and Calcutta. Film stars are admired and idolized. Indian films are shown mostly within the country, but they are exported also, especially to other countries in Asia and Africa.

Hockey is India's national sport. Spectators also enjoy football, basketball, volleyball, and cricket.

Above: The sun breaks through clouds over the Himalaya.
Below: There are about seventy sets of ghats, or steps, that lead down to the Ganges River, so that the faithful may bathe in its waters.

THE FUTURE

Mahatma Gandhi dreamed an impossible dream and lived long enough to see it come true. He believed that determination and nonviolent resistance were weapons that could win out over armed strength. He led millions of unorganized, undereducated, poverty-stricken people to resist the oppression of the world's largest empire.

A contemporary Indian poet, Namakkal Ramalingam Pillai, expresses his country's hope for the future in these words:

> Never forgetting Gandhi
> Never abandoning compassion,
> Never deviating from the path of
> Truth and peace,
> Let our country's freedom
> Be a beaconlight
> Unto all mankind.

Map Key

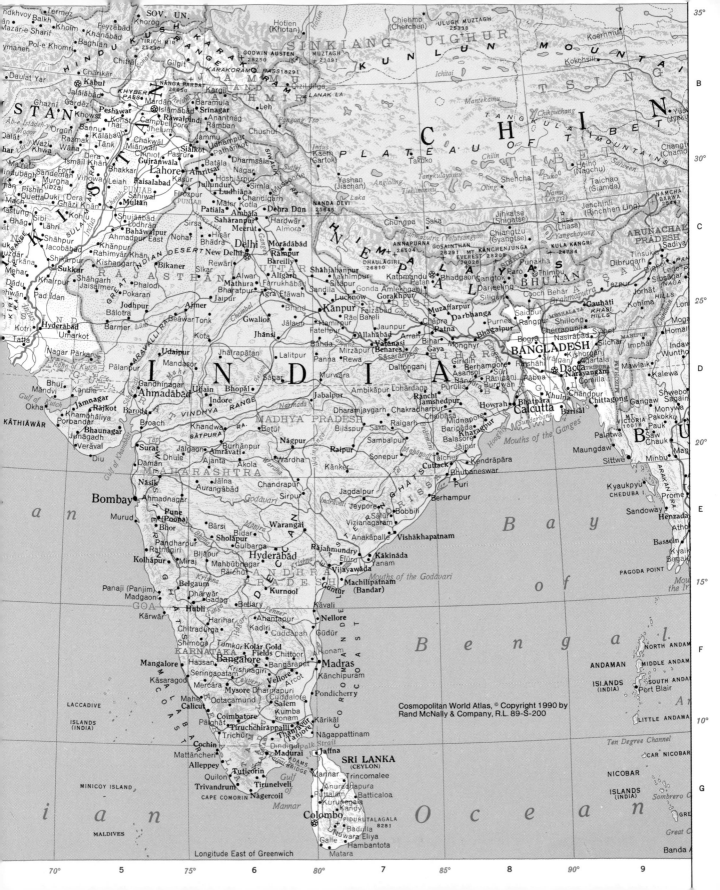

MINI-FACTS AT A GLANCE

GENERAL INFORMATION

Official Name: Bharat (Union of India)

Capital: New Delhi

Official Language: Hindi. English is widely used in government and it is called the associate official language. In addition, the following other languages have received official recognition in the constitution: Assamese, Bengali, Gujarati, Kannada, Malayan, Marathi, Oriya, Punjabi, Sanskrit, Sindhi, Tamil, Telugu, and Urdu.

Government: India's system of government evolved over 90 years of direct British rule. It is a parliamentary democracy. In 1947, after the British agreed to give India its independence, a constituent assembly elected by the provincial assemblies framed a constitution that came into force on January 26, 1950. All citizens of India who are 21 or older are eligible to vote.

The president, the vice-president, and the council of ministers under the prime minister constitute the executive branch. As in Great Britain, it is the prime minister who actually governs.

Parliament consists of an upper house, the *Rajya Sabha* or council of states, and a lower house, the *Lok Sabha* or house of the people. The Lok Sabha has most of the power. The number of seats for each state is proportionate to its population. The Rajya Sabha has a maximum membership of 250, of which all but 12 are elected by the state legislative assemblies. The others are nominated by the president in recognition of their contributions to literature, science, and social service.

Apart from a brief period between March 1977 and January 1980, India has been governed since independence by the Indian National Congress.

Religion: The overwhelming majority of Indians are classified as Hindu, though Hinduism includes a wide range of beliefs. In addition there are several other religious groups indigenous to India: the Sikhs, who are found mostly in Punjab; the Jains; and the Buddhists. Of the religions whose origin is not Indian, Islam has the largest number of adherents.

Flag: The national flag, adopted in 1947, is a tricolor of deep saffron, white, and green horizontal stripes. In the center of the white stripe is a blue wheel representing the wheel that appears on Asoka's lion capital at Sarnath, Uttar Pradesh; it is called the chakra, which comes from ancient Indian art and stands for the law of dharma.

National Anthem: *"Jana-gana-mana"* ("Thou Art the Ruler of the Minds of All People")

Money: The basic unit is the rupee (R). In October, 1990, 18.52 rupees were equal to one U.S. dollar.

Weights and Measures: Metric weights and measures, introduced in 1958, replaced the British and local systems.

Population: 853,373,000 (1990 estimate); 72 percent rural, 28 percent urban

Cities:

Bombay	8,243,405
Delhi	4,884,234
Calcutta	3,305,006
Madras	3,276,622
Bangalore	2,476,355
Hyderabad	2,150,058
Ahmadabad	2,059,725
Kanpur	1,481,789
Nagpur	1,219,461
Pune	1,203,351

(Population based on 1981 census.)

GEOGRAPHY

Highest point: Mount Kanchenjunga, 28,208 ft. (8,598 m)

Lowest point: Sea level along the coast

Rivers: The Ganges dominates India; it is one of three major river systems. It joins the Brahmaputra, which flows southward from Assam and forms a single major delta system in Bangladesh emptying into the Bay of Bengal.

Mountains: Some of the highest mountains in the world are found in the Himalaya, which extend 1,500 mi. (2,414 km) southward from the Afghanistan border and curve around the head of the Assam valley on the border of northeastern India and continue southward into Burma. The 4,000-ft. (1,219-m) Vindhya Range separates the southern peninsula from the northern plains.

Climate: India has a warm climate dominated by the seasonal winds known as monsoons, but differences in elevation and proximity to the oceans cause many variations in climate.

There are three seasons: In winter (November to February), temperatures range from 70° F. (21.1° C) and above in the south, in the 60s F. (15.5 to 21° C) in the plains, and the 40s and below (4.4° C and below) in the highlands. The hot season (March to May) is generally dry, windy, and dusty with temperatures rising to about 100° F. (37.7° C) in the plains. The monsoon season starts in June and continues through September. Cool weather begins in October.

Greatest Distances: North to south—2,000 mi. (3,219 km)
East to west—1,700 mi. (2,740 km)

Coastline: 4,252 mi. (6,843 km)

Area: 1,269,219 sq. mi. (3,287,263 km²)

NATURE

Trees: About one-fourth of the country is forested. In the western Himalaya vegetation changes with altitude from temperate deciduous forests at low elevations through coniferous forests to Alpine vegetation above the tree line. The eastern Himalaya have more extensive deciduous forest cover. In northeastern India vegetation cover ranges from tropical evergreen in the wet lowlands to temperate deciduous forest in drier and cooler areas. The semi-arid Punjab-Rajasthan-Gujarat region mainly supports scrub vegetation cover. In the heavily cultivated Ganges Plain, islands of deciduous trees and tuft grasses can be found. The peninsular uplands support deciduous and scrub forest, while the wetter slopes of the western Ghats support a tropical deciduous forest.

Animals: India has about 500 species of animals that include elephants, Indian bison, rhinoceroses, panthers, bears, antelope, wild goats and sheep, and tigers, which live mainly in the west, forested regions; the Himalayan markhors (ibexes) and lions live in the Gir forest. The government has created 247 wildlife sanctuaries and 53 national parks. The population of cattle, goats, buffalo, and sheep is the largest in the world, but the animals are malnourished and produce little milk.

Birds: There are more than 2,000 species of birds.

Fish: India is now fourth in Asia and eighth in the world in total fish production. The major fish caught are herring, sardines, and anchovies; flounder, halibut, and sole; tuna, bonito, and mackerel; and crustaceans. About two-thirds of the catch is sold fresh; one-fourth is sun dried.

EVERYDAY LIFE

Food: The Indian diet is varied. Jains do not eat meat, nor do many Hindus and Buddhists. Muslims eat meat, but not pork. Indians eat grains such as barley, rice, and wheat, and vegetables such as beans and peas. In northern India bread is made by grinding grain into flour and making dough. In southern India rice or vegetable seeds are soaked in water, made into a paste, and then made into dumplings.

Curry is one of the most popular dishes. Eggs, fish, meat, or vegetables are cooked in a spicy sauce. *Kabob* (pieces of meat grilled on skewers) and *kooftah* (ground meat with spices) are served often.

Coconut milk is enjoyed by many Indians.

Housing: Village houses are usually made of mud and reinforced with straw. Most daily activities take place outside on a veranda or in a courtyard. Many houses have electricity but no running water.

Holidays

January 26, Republic Day
August 15, Independence Day
October 2, Gandhi's Birthday
November 14, Nehru's Birthday

Culture: There has been a vigorous promotion of the arts in the years since independence. A revival of Indian folk painting and a new interest in the traditional schools of painting have both taken place. Architecture and sculpture have built on magnificent ancient and medieval traditions and have found new expressions with the introduction of Western influences.

The basis for all the arts is the great body of Vedic literature. The great Sanscrit epics—the *Mahabharata* and the *Ramayana*—were told orally for generations before they were written down.

The Mughal period saw the flourishing of literature, calligraphy, and book illustration.

It was Rabindranath Tagore who forged the link between tradition and modernity. The recipient of the Nobel Prize for Literature in 1913, he is the most important figure in modern Indian arts and literature. Of the more than 57,000 libraries in India, 190 have been declared to be of national importance. India ranks third as a publisher of books in the English language.

Traditional handicrafts—textiles, wood and ivory carving, metalware, and pottery—are being revived for export. They reflect the Indian love of ornamentation. Some of the finest objects come from Kashmir—papier-mâché, crewel embroidery, ivories, silverware, carpets, and shawls.

In the performing arts there is a renewed interest in classical Indian music and in regional dance forms. Ravi Shankar is the foremost Indian sitar player in the world. Western music and dance forms, radio, and television have risen in popularity. A large film industry has developed in Bombay and Madras.

Sports and Recreation: Sports do not occupy a prominent position in India, which has never won an Olympic gold medal. Hockey, badminton, wrestling, and lawn tennis have been somewhat popular, however.

Communication: Since independence India's press has enjoyed a high degree of freedom, except during the period from 1975-77 when a state of emergency was decreed. There are a large number of newspapers because of the diversity of languages, but few of them have large circulations. Because literacy is less than 40 percent, radio and television are the most influential media; both are operated by a state monopoly.

Transportation: The Indian railway system can be called the greatest in the world—it has the most trains, the most stations, and the most passengers. There are also about 5,000 mi. (8,047 km) of inland waterways. In addition to the major rivers—the Brahmaputra, the Ganges, the Godavari, and the Krishna—canals connect smaller rivers on the coastal plain.

Air traffic is served by several international and 99 domestic airports. It is the virtual monopoly of two public corporations, Air India and Indian Airlines—Air India operates internationally, Indian Airlines domestically.

The highway system has been enlarged and improved in recent years. But many roads are still poor in quality, and long-distance travel by automobile is still difficult. Vehicles pulled by animals or men, two-wheeled ox carts, and bicycles are still common modes of transportation.

Schools: Education is the concurrent responsibility of the national and state governments; the national government lays down policy directions and the states direct them. Primary education is free and compulsory for the 6-to-11 age group. Literacy has risen steadily; it is generally higher in urban areas. Most children of well-to-do parents attend private day schools or boarding schools. Village children attend school irregularly or not at all. They are needed in the fields or to help with younger children in the family. In 1986 Parliament authorized a national system of education whose goal is to provide free and compulsory education by 1995 for all children up to the age of 14.

There are more than 3,000 colleges of arts and sciences, as well as 215 medical colleges and over 100 institutions devoted to engineering and technology. Adult education and the reduction of illiteracy are major objectives.

Health and Welfare: In general state governments provide health-care facilities, and the national government sponsors and finances programs dealing with epidemic diseases and diseases resulting from nutritional deficiencies. Many new hospitals and clinics have been built since the 1950s. Malaria, tuberculosis, cholera, dysentery, and influenza plague the country; malnutrition is a serious problem.

The delivery of welfare services is the responsibility of both the central and state governments. It aims to provide relief and rehabilitation to the handicapped and to women and children, particularly those from the needier sections of society.

ECONOMY AND INDUSTRY

Principal Products:
Agriculture: Peanuts, cashews, rice, pepper, sugarcane, tea, coffee, vegetables, wheat, linseed, cotton, jute, tobacco
Manufacturing and Processing: Brass ware and silverware, jute bags and rope, leather goods, woodwork, rayon, rugs, drugs, sugar, fertilizer, cement, chemicals, cotton and silk materials, electric motors, iron and steel, paper
Mining: salt, iron ore, silver, manganese ore, bauxite, mica, chromite, copper, gold, lead, coal, precious and semi-precious stones

IMPORTANT DATES

c. 2500 B.C.—Civilization begins to flourish in the Indus valley

c. 1500—Aryans invade India and dominate for 500 years

518—King Darius I of Persia invades northwest India

500 B.C. to A.D. 800—Buddhism becomes widespread, but finally gives way to Hinduism

327 B.C.—Alexander the Great overthrows Darius III. His Indian campaign opens up routes between Europe and the subcontinent of India

A.D. 320-c. 750—Gupta Dynasty unifies northern India

1200—A network of Hindu kingdoms covers the subcontinent

1206—First Islamic dynasty in South Asia is established

1498—Vasco da Gama of Portugal reaches India

1526—Mughal Empire is established by Babar, the Muslim leader of Kabul; Mughals rule until 1707

1542—First Christian missionary, Saint Francis Xavier, arrives

1600—East India Company is chartered by Queen Elizabeth of England

1608—East India Company ships arrive

1757—British East India Company gains control of Bengal

1774—Warren Hastings, the first British governor-general, takes office

1818—British establish control over most of the subcontinent

1857-59—British crush the Sepoy Mutiny, the "First War of Independence"

1858—British government takes over the rule of India from the East India Company

1869—Mohandas K. Gandhi is born

1870s—Indian independence movement begins to grow

1885—Indian National Congress is founded

1906—Muslim League is organized

1917—Parliament declares that self-government is its aim for India

1920—Gandhi becomes leader of the Indian National Congress party and starts a program of nonviolent disobedience against the British

1922—Gandhi imprisoned for civil disobedience

1929—Jawaharlal Nehru is elected president of Indian National Congress

1930—Gandhi leads protest against salt tax

1935—Britain passes the Government of India Act, outlining a framework for self-government of India

1939—World War II begins in Europe

1940—Muslim League demands that a separate Muslim country, Pakistan, be carved out of India

1947—India becomes independent on August 15, the day after Pakistan is created; both become members of the British Commonwealth

1947-49—India and Pakistan fight over Kashmir

1948—Gandhi is fatally shot

1950—India adopts a new constitution and becomes first republic in the British Commonwealth

1964—Nehru dies

1966—Indira Gandhi, Jawaharlal Nehru's daughter, becomes India's first woman prime minister

1971—India assists East Pakistan in war against West Pakistan. West Pakistan is defeated and East Pakistan becomes the independent nation of Bangladesh

1974—India explodes its first atomic bomb

1975—Prime Minister Indira Gandhi's government begins censoring the press and arrests many political opponents

1977—Gandhi and her Congress party are defeated in parliamentary elections

1980—Indira Gandhi and her new Congress party are reelected

1984—Indira Gandhi is assassinated; her son, Rajiv Gandhi, succeeds her

1989—Vishwanath Pratap Singh becomes prime minister

1991—World leaders condemn the assassination of Rajiv Gandhi, former Prime Minister, at an election rally; the Congress party wins a plurality of votes in the general elections and names Narasimha Rao as prime minister

IMPORTANT PEOPLE

Akbar (1542-1605), grandson of Babar, the greatest Mughal ruler, a wise and successful leader

Asoka (c. 265-238 or c. 273-232 B.C.), the last emperor of the Mauryan Dynasty

Aurangzeb (1618-1707), the sixth Mughal emperor of Hindustan

Babar (1483-1530), founder of Mughal Dynasty who invaded India in 1526

Annie W. Besant (1847-1933), English theosophist, author, and Indian leader

Bhavabhuti (c. A.D. 736-?), Sanskrit dramatist

Chandragupta I of Maurya Dynasty (321 B.C. -?), established an empire extending over much of northern India

Chandragupta II of Gupta Dynasty (c. 380-c. 415), founded another empire across northern India

Robert Clive (1725-74), British soldier and founder of the empire of British India

Lord Charles Cornwallis (1738-1805), governor-general of the East India Company

Indira Gandhi (1917-84), daughter of Jawaharlal Nehru, prime minister from 1966-77 and 1980-84; assassinated

Mohandas K. Gandhi (1869-1948), called Mahatma; Hindu nationalist and spiritual leader

Harsha (c. 590-c. 647), king of northern India

Warren Hastings (1732-1818), English statesman and administrator in India

Jahangir (1569-1627), son of Akbar, brought Persian influence into India

Muhammad Ali Jinnah (1876-1948), president of the Muslim League, first governor-general of Pakistan

Kanishka (-Second Century A.D.), king of India, adopted Buddhism

Rudyard Kipling (1865-1936), English writer, born in India

Nanak (1469-1538), called Guru; founder of religion known as Sikhism

Jawaharlal Nehru (1889-1964), India's first prime minister after independence

Sir Chandrasekhara V. Raman (1888-1970), Indian physicist and author

Shah Jahan (1592-1666), Jahangir's successor, builder of the Taj Mahal

Siddhartha Gautama, (c. 563-c. 483 B.C.), called Buddha; Indian philosopher, founder of Buddhism

Sir Rabindranath Tagore (1861-1941), world-famous writer and artist, winner of Nobel Prize for literature in 1913, resigned knighthood in 1919

Mother Teresa (1910-   ), called "Saint of the Gutters"; Roman Catholic nun, originally from Yugoslavia, winner of the Nobel Prize in 1979 for her work with the poor in India

Archibald P. Wavell (1883-1950), commander-in-chief of British forces in India, viceroy of India from 1943-47

Saint Francis Xavier (1506-52), first Christian missionary to India

INDEX

Page numbers that appear in boldface type indicate illustrations

About the Author

Sylvia McNair is the author of numerous books for adults and young people about interesting places. Her articles on travel, education, and other subjects appear regularly in national magazines. A graduate of Oberlin College, she has toured all fifty of the United States, as well as more than thirty foreign countries on six continents. She was born in Korea, and says that Asian countries are especially fascinating to her.

"We have much to learn from India," she says. "It is one of the oldest civilizations in the world, and I hope that American young people will become increasingly interested in learning about it."

Sylvia McNair lives in Evanston, Illinois. She has three sons, one daughter, and two grandsons.